Thinking aloud. It's something I've always done — much to the dismay of many. Then one day, a good friend who is also a publisher asked me to turn my penchant for stream-of-consciousness commentary on anything and everything into a column for his newspaper. "The world's a mess. Make my readers smile," he said, adding quickly that I was to "keep it clean and not get too snarky." He even had one of his artists do a little caricature of me, which, not surprisingly, has only a mouth. So that's what I do — every week, and while I do shoot for those smiles, there are times when what I write prompts something else.

Sometimes, it's a little optimism or hope, and sometimes it's reflection or a tear. I've been known to irritate, though that's never my intention. I'm guessing I'm responsible for more than a few yawns. And I know I have, on occasion, raised genuine concerns about my sanity. But in between are smiles — and even a few laughs, or so I'm told. And so, at the encouragement of my official fan club, which is rapidly closing in on double-digit membership (though six are close relatives), here they all are. So far, anyway. Three years of *Thinking Aloud*.

Results may vary. Enjoy in moderation.

Judy

© 2013, Judith S. Henderson, All Rights Reserved

Table of Contents

Heard the News? 9
Apparently, I Missed the Memo 10
Five of My Favorite Minutes 11
Bathrobes and Other Benchmarks of Independence 12
Fond Memories of One Week, Three Channels, and No Bill 13
Name That Tune 14
I'm Starting to Miss My Toes 15
Give Pieces a Chance 16
Food for Thought 17
New Shoes and a Box of Pencils Do Not an Anthill Make 18
Hats Off to the Ladies of Great Britain 19
The Haunting 20
My Tree People 21
Homeless Hardware 22
The Reunion 23
The Pony in the Manure 24
Welcome to the Big Table 25
Parking the Dog 26
Turkey O'clock at Gobbler's Drift 27
My New Cost-of-Living Diet 28
When Words Fail 29
Who Gets to be First? 30
The Fungus Among Us 31
Yes, Virginia, There is an Easter Bunny 32
It's Not the Dishes. It's the Dishes. 33
Pills vs. Pillows 34
Stop and Go 35
Mums the Word 36
Freeze Frames 37
December 23rd, Thursdays, and March 38
Thank Goodness 39
Congratulations are in Order 40
The Two-Dog Two Step 41
The Wicked Witch of the Yard 42

It's Official. I'm Invisible. 43
One Soldier. Immeasurable Thanks. 44
A Little Must is a Big Must 46
Jergen's Law 47
Exclamation Points 48
I'm Sorry. It Must be Said. 49
Sometimes I Wonder 50
I Am Becoming My Mother 51
Winter Blossoms 52
Going Topless 53
It's a Wrap 54
I Could be a Winner 55
Junk Drawers, Poltergeists, and Other Rationalizations 56
Cell Phones, Darwin, and a Thing Called eVolution 57
DNDIY 58
Sometimes, Default is Our Own 59
Life After Death 60
Twelve days of Tinsel 61
Talking Tees 62
Do Not Call 63
My Food Channel Moment 64
Tricky Treats 65
Spandex 66
Many Happy Returns 67
Spring Songs and Blue Toes 68
Nine Eleven 69
In Gratitude for Weeds 70
Lighten Up 71
Saved by the Nut with the Dogs 72
I Do Not Love Valentine's Day 73
Dog People 74
Let's Get Real 75
Grid and Bear It 76
Hard-Wired Memories 77
Hmmmmmmm… 78
How to Live to be 100 79
My Little Bug's Little Bug was Bugging Me a Little 80

Bird Feeders. World Peace. And Squirrels. 81
Summer Sounds 82
I Give Up 83
Leaf Envy 84
I've Had Qwite a Revelation 85
Ah, the Wonders of Nature 86
Finally. It is Spring. 87
Neighbors 88
Just Say Whoa! 89
Lefty Loosey. Righty Tighty. 90
I Could be Getting Old 91
I Have a Confession to Make 92
My Tree. My Roots. 93
Led Zeppelin: Now Appearing in Baked Goods 94
Things are Not Looking Up at Downton Abbey 95
Hat Hair 96
Paul McCartney Got Married. Again. 97
The Good Humor Man 98
January Means Back to Normal 99
The Walk 100
Our Blessed Event 101
What Is It About Jelly Beans? 102
Brain Songs 103
Another Nine Eleven 104
The Holidays are Here! 106
Moving 107
Nature's Grand Finale 108
Mosquitoes 109
My Box of Dirt 110
American Idle 111
The Real Flower Power 112
The Kid Across the Street 113
Happy Hannukah 114
It's a Dog's Life 115
Enjoy Your Trip? 116
In Sympathy and Hope 117
What Goes Up Must Come Down 118

The Blessing of Spaghetti 119
Sleeping with a Skunk 120
Smooth Talkers 121
The Children Between the Headlines 122
Technologeez! 124
Fried Green Tomato 125
Weighty Thoughts 126
Aha! 127
The Switch 128
Weeds and Wildflowers 129
Seeing is Relieving 130
The Nightly Ews 131
Infinity and Plastic Wrap 132
…And Yet, We Still Live in New England 133
Why Is It? 134
The Late Judith Henderson 135
Heart Lines 136
Well, This Could Spell Trouble 138
I'll Be Back 139
Canine Sleep Deprivation 140
So I Said to My Husband… 142
Forget the NSA 143
My New Years Resolutions 144
Cents and Sensibility 145
The First Day of Spring 146
The Bottom-Shelf Rancid Red Blues 148
Meandering the Mall 149
They Rod and Thy Staff — and Hal, They Comfort Me 150
Deck the Halls with Boughs of Holly? 152
Nobody Touches the Krud Kutter 153
The Laundry on the Stairs 154
Late Life Lyrics 155
Thesaurus Anyone? 156
In the Black 157
She of the Stupid Hat 158
I'm Thankful For What I *Don't* Have 159

Thinking Aloud

Heard the News?

The Rolling Stones are hitting the road for a 50th Anniversary Tour, and so are the Beach Boys. (That's right, 50th — as in five oh-my-god.) So, is it just me or are there other Baby Boomers out there wondering how that is even possible? I mean, did I — did *we* — miss something, like a decade or three? Frankly, the whole thing is making me feel old, and that, in turn, is making me feel cranky. So will I be going to one of these 50th anniversary concerts? I don't think so.

For starters, the tickets don't come cheap, requiring either a small home equity loan or the sale of some family jewelry. For another, I can't stay awake that late anymore. And finally, I like my rock stars frozen in time. I learned that one warm summer night, when a lead singer I've lusted after forever emerged from his tour bus looking his age — and then some. (If only I hadn't been wearing my glasses.)

Anyway, I wish them all luck — and their audiences, too.

I'll be home remembering when...

Apparently, I Missed the Memo

You know, the one about not having to actually *use* your blinker in advance of making a turn anymore. The one that must have said something like "If you manage to activate your blinker one millisecond or less before you actually execute your turn, good for you" — then added "but if you forget entirely…oh well." And I began suspecting that I missed that particular memo yesterday, after having no less than four cars in front of me come to a mysterious stop, then turn right or left. Three didn't activate their blinkers until after beginning their turns. The fourth didn't bother, period.

Now, call me crazy, but I was taught that the blinker was there to signal one's intentions — you know, give the poor soul behind you some sense of what you are about to do, especially if it involves braking and even more especially if it involves braking completely. So, memo or no memo, I shall continue signaling. That one-finger flip is the best way I know of to avoid another, though slightly different, one-finger flip often seen in one's rear view mirror at surprisingly close range following the screech of brakes.

I might even live longer…

Five of my Favorite Minutes

OK, I'm not really proud of this — but given how look-at-me-look-at-me so many of our celebrities are these days, I do get a kick out of the five minutes I spend waiting to go through the check-out line at the grocery store. Why? Because that's when I can get a good look at the cheesy tabloids that are full of celebrity "oops" shots — and that kind of does my heart good.

These stars-without-make-up photos remind me that the only difference between us and them is a hair stylist, a make-up artist, and, when all is said and downloaded, an air-brushing specialist capable of fixing whatever the first two missed. And as someone who, at least at this point in my life, would not be caught dead romping on a beach in anything less than a full-length prom dress with sleeves, it's every-so-slightly gratifying to see that when caught unawares in ill-advised bikinis and speedos, our Hollywood royalty have either cellulite in their thighs, muffin tops for waists, triggles under their arms, or doolaps beneath their chins. Sometimes all four!

Am I mean-spirited? No. At least I hope not. But I *will* admit that I am relieved at knowing that we are all in the same boat.

The only real difference is that for us, it's a just figure of speech — and for them it's a yacht…

Bathrobes and Other Benchmarks of Independence

Until now, I had never actually bought myself a bathrobe because bathrobes seemed to be something my mother always bought — first out of necessity but eventually because it was such a good Christmas gift. Same thing with winter coats. Indeed, every few years, my mother would say, "You could use a new winter coat…" and off we'd go to do a little shopping followed by lunch. When she died, there were so many things I missed about her, but new robes and coats were not among them.

Well, last year — five years after her going, I took one look at my tired old bathrobe and another at my sad old winter coat, and for the very first time ever I realized that I was really and truly on my own. So what did I do? I did what she taught me to do. I said to myself, "You could use a new robe and a new winter coat…." Then I took myself shopping and I treated myself to lunch.

Call me crazy, but I swear I wasn't alone…

Fond Memories of One Week, Three Channels, and No Bill

Recently, I found myself thinking about what the fall TV season was like when I was a kid, and I've decided that it was much better than today's. Every new show from all three networks — OK, the *only* three networks — debuted during one exciting week. Now, shows come and go as quickly as my hot flashes, making it impossible to either keep up or get hooked.

I suppose the thing that bugs me the most is that out of three networks that didn't cost a cent, there was always something worth watching. Now, armed with more than a hundred channels (and exactly twice that number if you go backwards hoping for different shows — which is something I tend to do despite having a college degree), I can never find anything good to watch. "We pay for this," I say to my husband as we search for something to watch. "I know," says he. Then, after a short pause, he suggests I try going the other way.

Thank God for that remote...

Name That Tune

I have two weird and largely useless talents. I remember *all* of the words to *all* of the songs I've ever heard, including commercial jingles and movie and sitcom theme songs. And I remember *all* of the tunes.

Now, there are those who would say, "Cool!" But this *song savant* thing isn't actually cool unless you're blessed with both a good memory for lyrics and melodies *and* a good voice — and I was not. As a result, my husband has had to endure me singing along with every song I hear since shortly after uttering the words *I do*.

Well, love may be blind — but it's not deaf. And so, in a very gracious effort to orchestrate a well-deserved and psychologically necessary break from my ongoing concert, he recently presented me with a cool little iPod Shuffle with its equally cool little ear buds, obviously hoping they might unite me and my music quietly in the privacy of my head. But sadly, it did not work out that way. I simply became the *only* singer he could hear. It's OK, though.

He now has his own iPod Shuffle, and you can bet that if I'm listening to mine, he's got his turned up...

I'm Starting to Miss My Toes

With eligibility for my senior discount bearing down on me like a train without brakes, I have to say that this aging thing really isn't all that bad. I'm not crazy about the way my skin has started to resemble seersucker, and I do wish I could still squat without needing something sturdy to hang onto in order to get up — but that's all minor.

What's not so minor are the reading glasses scattered everywhere, some of which are for nothing more than finding the others. They range in strength from 1.5 (the good old days) to 3.25 (my latest, bought to read a certain book set in what I hope is smaller type than usual), and for the most part, they get me through the day. But whenever it's time for a do-it-myself pedicure, there's simply no denying it. I cannot see my toes. They are too close for the distance glasses, too distant for the readers, and, as we already know, I can no longer squat.

I shall miss them...

Give Pieces a Chance

I know it takes a lot of different people to make potato chips. There are the people to grow the potatoes and people to harvest them. There are people to sort out the bad ones — which, when sliced, might resemble things no food should resemble — and people to slice the rest. There are people to fry or bake them, people to salt or season them, and people to get them safely into their brightly colored bags. There are even people to ensure that at least half of that bag is filled with air, thus allowing the chips to settle and profits to soar. But who stomps on each bag just before it goes out the door?

Someone does. Someone *must*, given the abundance of crushed chips found just beneath each top layer of survivors, superbly whole and crisp, having escaped the carnage. I just want to know in my heart that bags full of air and pulverized snack food have a higher purpose which I, as a consumer, cannot possibly understand but which is clear to those more connected with the Universe.

Otherwise, I might be a little irritated...

Food for Thought

Anyone who really cares about eating healthy has a tendency to pay close attention to the so-called experts on such things. I know I always have. Indeed, long before low-fat foods were available commercially, I was making my own. (That would, of course, explain why — in a desperate albeit misguided effort to give my low-fat spaghetti sauce some actual flavor — I used progressively hotter and hotter peppers until it became necessary to add chapstick and kleenex to every place setting at the dinner table.)

Anyway, I'm done listening, because it seems like all the advice they give us gets retracted or significantly modified — eventually. And sometimes, after we've long since sworn off a particular food or ingredient, we are told that it might actually be beneficial. Last week alone, the CDC noted that salt may not be so bad in moderation. Indeed, too little can be unhealthy. (Really? Thanks.) And another study noted that those huge doses of fish oil supplements everyone's been taking to stay heart healthy could be a precipitating factor in prostate cancer. (Great!) So I'm done. I'll eat what I want — in moderation, of course.

God forbid the CDC should suddenly announce that the key to immortality is a diet rich in cheesecake and I haven't had any...

New Shoes and a Box of Pencils Do Not an Ant Hill Make

I hate to see the summer end. But then, I've always hated to see summer end — even when I was little.

As a kid, I loved sleeping late and awakening naturally to a whole day filled with absolutely nothing to do but whatever I *wanted* to do — like lying under a tree on my stomach watching the ants in the grass or lying under a tree on my back watching the clouds in the sky. Indeed, with summer an endless stretch of just such days, summer was my season — right up until August 1st, when ads for back-to-school supplies and clothes evoked the dark specter of early mornings and stuffy classrooms.

Oh sure. There were new school shoes, all scuff-free and shiny…the annual box of No. 2 pencils embossed with my full name in glorious gold…and a cool new lunchbox destined to smell like peanut butter and apples. But those things were cold comfort for someone enchanted by ants. There's good news, though.

You can still watch clouds through a schoolroom window — and October really isn't too early to begin thinking about next summer…

Hats Off to the Ladies of Great Britain

No, really. I'm serious. Please take off those hats! British fashion experts may call them *fascinators*, but my trusty online Urban Dictionary defines these fascinators as "a concoction of feathers, lace, and random dead birds," and frankly, I have to agree.

I mean, there I was, up at dawn and ready to savor all the pomp and circumstance of Will and Kate's royal wedding, when the parade of hazardous hats began. In no time at all, my joyful anticipation turned to fear that the Duchess of Whatever might turn suddenly, skewering the eye of the poor soul seated beside her and causing others nearby, sporting equally menacing hats, to turn suddenly, as well — all with similar results, thus ruining an otherwise glorious spectacle in, well… the blink of an eye! Thankfully, that did not happen, but there's always a next time. And so, to England's noble ladies, I say hats off.

And *do* be careful where you put them…

The Haunting

I watch *Ghost Hunters* — and have for years, so when we moved into our new home and a glow began appearing above my husband's bureau late at night, I noticed. I even got up several times to see if a reflection from outside were causing it. But there was no reflection. Just that glow.

"Our house is haunted," I told my husband. "No it's not," he said. "Then explain the glow," I replied — to which he responded, "Do we have any cookies?"

Well, when the glow reappeared that very night, I decided I'd had enough, marched over to that bureau fully prepared to confront the unknown, and discovered that our nightly apparition was actually my husband's electric razor, lying hidden behind a family photo for its nightly recharge — a tiny little "ready" light emitting not just *a* glow but *the* glow.

Seems it wasn't a haunting after all — just a close shave…

My Tree People

Housekeeping is dull. In fact, it is *so* dull that I often amuse myself by figuring out how many times I've done a particular chore to pass the time while doing that very same chore. For example, I know that I've cleaned nearly 5,000 bathrooms since moving to my first apartment, including the 840 or so additional cleanings prompted by holidays and other special occasions when guests were coming over. And I know that I have dusted the house roughly 2,552 times, including the 420 extra dustings that went with the 840 extra bathroom cleanings.

Well recently, while washing the dinner dishes for the 6,396th time, I discovered that if I squint while looking out at the woods, all of the leaves and branches form tiny faces! So now, instead of multiplying while I do dishes, I scrub and squint until the sink is empty and the woods are full — full of little tree people. Odd? Probably. But it beats doing all that math, which gives me a headache.

And frankly, I enjoy the company...

Homeless Hardware

Yesterday, after parking my car, I spotted a big, greasy bolt on the ground in the space next to mine, and — having a rather vivid worst-case-scenario kind of imagination — all I could think was, "Well, *that* can't be good. Somebody's out there right now stranded by the side of the road in a car whose engine fell out a hundred yards back." It also reminded me of the day my husband and I re-stepped the mast on our first little sailboat.

Determined to be self-sufficient, we'd taken it down by ourselves the previous fall, making detailed diagrams of where everything went and placing each piece of hardware into a small baggy that we guarded with our lives all winter. Unfortunately, once that mast was back up, we had two cotter pins and a screw left over.

"Well, *that* can't be good," I said to my husband, who, having rechecked the stays and collar ten times, had already moved on to lunch. "Don't worry about it," he said between bites. But I did, and for the next five months, I kept those dumb cotter pins and that stupid screw close at hand in case that mast let loose.

Amazingly, it never did — at least not that we knew about. At the end of the season, we sold the boat. Got a good price, too. But then why not? It wasn't just pristine.

It came with extra hardware...

The Reunion

I recently had the pleasure of attending my husband's high school reunion. I won't say which one, but because of the small (wink! wink!) age difference between us, I was prepared to feel like a kid. Wrong.

There I was, serving myself some creamed something-or-other in the buffet line when the gentleman in front of me turned, took a good long look at my face, then grinned. "Yeah…I remember you!" he said.

"I don't think so," I replied as cheerfully as I could, but he persisted, forcing me to note that I was actually in kindergarten the year he and his classmates graduated — and you know, you would have thought that would have been that, wouldn't you? But no. "Are you sure?" he asked. And he wasn't kidding.

"It's his eyesight," said my always-gallant husband when I returned to the table, my vanity in shambles. "He probably thought you were someone else." But I wasn't taking any chances. I got *myself* some glasses — and they were all filled with red wine! Fortunately, there was an open bar. I had a designated driver, too.

He was one very handsome guy who couldn't take me to his senior prom because it was past my bedtime — but made up for it by marrying me…

The Pony in the Manure

Optimism is everything. I thought about that yesterday as I was buying gas at more than $4 a gallon and happened to remember the story about the little boy and the manure.

Seems this kid's folks worried that he was just *too* optimistic, so the night before his birthday, they had a pile of manure delivered. No gifts. Just manure. "That should teach him that life isn't always wonderful," they thought — but when morning arrived, there he was, out in the yard, happily plowing through that pile of manure. And when they shrieked, "What are you doing?" — horrified at the sight of their precious child digging in the dung, the little boy responded, "I'm looking for the pony!"

Well, I thought about that. Then I thought about the price of gas. And you know what? I found the pony in the manure! Pumping 5 gallons at $4 takes half as long as pumping 5 gallons at $2.

And if the price gets high enough, I won't be pumping at all, giving me plenty of extra time to start looking for a horse…

Welcome to the Big Table

My niece graduated from college the other day. And next week her brother is graduating from high school. I'm just sitting here wondering how that is possible.

I remember the day she, who had the chubbiest little cheeks I've ever seen, fawned over her brand new baby brother, who was the spitting image of Charlie Brown — the delicate task of distributing Halloween candy equitably between siblings not yet having reared its ugly head. Then I blinked and here we are. She writes like a pro. He's studying business. And both have gone from cute as can be into really amazing people, graduating not only from their respective schools but from that kids' table every family has — if only symbolically.

There are just two things I want them to remember, now that they've joined the adults. The first is that while the main menu rarely changes, we look forward to the fresh new sides you will bring with you to expand our palates and open our minds. Second? It's your turn to help with the dishes.

Just remember that a clean sink is its own reward — and I'll always be here to dry…

Parking the Dog

Parking a dog is a little like parking a car, except that instead of squeezing a big metal hulk into a small space so that you can go do whatever *you* want to do, parking dogs involves unleashing small fur balls into a huge space so that they can go do whatever *they* want to do — and at a dog park, there's plenty to do!

Each visit begins with official greetings, during which there's a lot of sniffing, as well as the occasional growl when the sniffing gets too personal. Following that is a quick sweep of the grounds to determine who has, well…*been and gone*, as it were. Then it's on to the games, which include chasing the ball, chasing another dog with the ball, stealing the ball, burying the ball, guarding the ball, smelling the ball, barking at the ball, chewing the ball, and sometimes just staring at the ball. But you know. When it's time to leash up and head out, the good byes are surprisingly short and sweet. Apparently, there's just nothing better than home — home being where the heart is.

Of course, it's also where that cupboard with all the great treats is…

Turkey O'clock at Gobbler's Drift

A few years back, I arrived home at the end of a cold, February day to find my husband staring pensively into the woods. "Having a moment?" I asked. "No," said he. "I'm watching turkeys."

And so he was, our bare woods dotted with dozens and dozens of wild turkeys perched high, low, and everywhere in between. Indeed, from that day on, we'd go out at 5:00 p.m. sharp to watch the turkeys gather — and at precisely 5:15, up they'd fly into the trees, where they'd stay until dawn. Fortunately, we have witnesses — all family members we held hostage after one Sunday dinner to watch our miracle unfold, because soon after, the turkeys left, never to return.

Well, after that we took to calling our little house *Gobbler's Drift*, and for the longest time we found ourselves peeking into the woods around dusk. I mean, wild turkeys may not be much to look at but they are very punctual and oddly fascinating.

And while we never saw them again, for a little while one winter, we had the pleasure of setting our clocks by them…

My New Cost-of-Living Diet

Yesterday, I went to a fast food place to get a small milkshake only to be handed a miniature version of the last small milkshake I had bought at that same fast food place for the same price just a few months earlier. Well, I looked at it for a minute. Then drank it.

I drank it instead of complaining because almost everything I buy these days is smaller than it used to be, whether it's the package or the portion, a little cost-of-living sleight of hand retailers hope we won't notice as much as a price hike. (Note to retailers: We notice!) But you know, there's an upside to all this shrinkage.

It's like a clever new diet. And unless I start buying two of everything — which I can't afford to do, I should be down by at least ten pounds in no time.

Don't you just love silver linings…

When Words Fail

Sometimes — though, I admit, not often — I am left speechless. For example, I am left speechless whenever I see someone who absolutely should *not* be wearing a tube top wearing a tube top, and I am left speechless when another driver bolts out in front of me only to achieve no more than 21.3 miles per hour for the next five miles in a no-passing zone.

Likewise, I am left speechless by people having loud conversations into cell phone headsets I cannot see — and just the other day I was left speechless watching a woman transfer all of the best strawberries from two plastic containers into one, which she then bought, leaving the other filled with duds behind.

Well, when I told my husband I was writing this week's column about things that leave me speechless, he started laughing and said, "You know, in thirty years, I don't think I've ever actually seen you speechless."

He has now…

Who Gets to be First?

I always wonder about that whenever I have a repairman coming, since I've never had a repairman show up until one minute before my 8-to-noon or 1-to-5 window officially closes.

Of course, there are worse things than being held captive in one's own home, where having the time to catch up on a few chores or listen to the quiet can be wonderful! But I'm still curious. Who gets to be first? Someone must. And if someone does, then I want to know how he or she got to be first, as well as what someone who gets to be first does after being first.

Does he or she actually go back to work or just hang around awhile enjoying things, then lie to the boss about the repairman not showing up until 11:59 or 4:59? After all, who would know? I mean, no one I know has ever *gotten* to be first. And no one I know *knows* anyone who has ever gotten to be first, so who would know?

If I ever get to be first, I'll let you know...

The Fungus Among Us

I don't care how shady my yard is. The number of mushrooms and toadstools growing in various sizes, shapes, and colors under bushes, between flowers, and right out in the middle of the grass is just weird. More curious still is the fact that one minute they're not there — and then poof, they are. We've gathered bags of them only to turn around and find more sprouting in our wake.

Now, heaven knows I love a good stuffed or grilled portabella, but these fungi are not edible. Indeed, most are the poisonous kind used to finish off some poor, unwitting soul in a good Agatha Christie novel, so there's no stuffing or grilling to be done. Just picking and tossing and hand washing, which is getting old. It's also getting worrisome.

I'm a little concerned about how many faeries, trolls, devas, gnomes, and other little nature spirits are missing their little nature furniture — and if they know who took it…

Yes, Virginia,
There is an Easter Bunny

In fact, there are lots of Easter Bunnies. I know because my Dad was one of them!

The night before Easter, he'd spend hours hiding our candy — and while he was clever with everything from those marshmallow peeps to the little chocolate eggs, his genius with jelly beans was the stuff of legends.

He'd place one in each of the finger holes on all of our rotary-dial phones, one atop every plug in every wall socket, and dozens in the nooks and crannies of the dining room chandelier. He'd line them up on doorframes and window frames and picture frames. He'd even balance them on lamps and across the back of chairs and couches, rendering whole rooms useless for the rest of the night. And while he had a sharp eye and steady hand, more than a few hit the ground, rolling out of sight until one of us enterprising kids discovered it days, weeks, and sometimes even months later. Happily for us, jelly beans do not go bad or get stale. They just get a little fuzzy.

And if memory serves, a little fuzz doesn't actually interfere with the taste…

It's not the Dishes.
It's the Dishes.

I know. It's sound so negative. But anyone who has ever found themselves hosting the family's annual Thanksgiving gathering knows exactly what I'm talking about: Thanksgiving dinner is a pain.

It's not that cooking the meal is so hard. After your first few Thanksgivings, that naked turkey isn't particularly daunting, nor is the long, long list of favorite dishes that absolutely *must* be included on the menu — even though it grows every time someone new marries into the family, even though only one person actually eats those nasty turnips, and even though nobody (and I mean *nobody*) knows what's in mince pie. It's the dishes *after* those dishes.

There are hundreds of them. Maybe even thousands. OK, that might be an exaggeration, but all I know is this. It's not the tryptophan in the turkey causing the coma that overtakes everyone following dessert. It's knowing that anyone still conscious after dinner gets to do those dishes.

Zzzzz…

Pills vs. Pillows

I love pillows. And I love pillows because the right new pillow can change my whole mood! That said, too many can render a couch completely useless— which I happen to know because I have just such a couch.

Overstuffed and a little over-the-top, thanks to no less than five coordinating fabrics, it's frivolous and fun. In fact, it's so frivolous and fun, that I used to have two equally overstuffed, over-the-top pillows poised at each end. I still think they made the whole thing look like the softest, happiest place on earth — but any attempt to actually *sit* on it left guests foundering helplessly in a sea of eiderdown, so I've had to cut back. Now, two modest pillows punctuate my sofa like two little parentheses, dull but useful. However, I am pleased to note that my bedroom remains home to seven pillows bursting with feathers and colors, which always make me smile.

Seems one sure cure for feeling a little down is, well… feeling a little down — and when I'm blue, adding a little yellow, some green, and a bit of pink works wonders…

Stop and Go

Walking my dogs is not exercise. I wish it were, but it's not, and that's because there are no less than 43 other dogs in our neighborhood — all of whom we know — so when we walk, my two insist on stopping at precise six-foot intervals to sniff every blade of grass, every grain of sand, every leaf or stick, and every drop of rain or flake of snow within reach for whatever pee-mail might have been left by the last of their friends to pass by. Only when they are satisfied that they know precisely which of those 43 other dogs they will be addressing and how they want to reply do they finally piddle their answer — and on we go. For another six feet.

Sometimes, I wonder just what these messages say. "Warm welcome?" "Urine my thoughts?" "Yellow there!" Who knows. But I do know one thing. At the end of each walk, my little ones are completely exhausted and ready for a nap.

I, however, have gained another pound…

Mums the Word

You know, every April, I await the return of my perennials with genuine anticipation, and when May arrives, I actually count heads. In June, I watch in awe as they grow and bud. In July, all the bright colors punctuating summer's lush greens make me wonder how I ever survive winter. But by August, I am done.

Partly, it's the heat and humidity, and partly it's the droopers. (You know, those flowers that demand constant watering — the horticultural equivalent of whiney children.) But it's also because that's when both weeds and mosquitoes thrive.

Then comes September, and with it, cooler days, fewer bugs — and the autumn garden. And while the authentic autumn garden "experience" should include a quaint roadside stand, some cider, a bushel of apples, and at least one baked good made with cider or apples, the truth is, you don't need the experience. You just need the mums, which can be purchased almost anywhere.

Hey — a mum is mum is a mum, so if you're mum about where your mums come from, it's all good...

Freeze Frames

Like most people, my mind is filled with memories of family and friends, schools, places I've lived and visited, old boyfriends, cherished pets, books — even long-discarded furniture and clothes. But some memories stand out, unusually vivid in their clarity like brilliant freeze frames in an otherwise indistinct video.

I have one incredibly detailed memory of zipping my first little dog *Woofer* into my parka on our way home from a terribly cold late-night piddle — and another of me clinging tearfully to my father as he and my mother struggled to make their getaway from my freshman dorm parking lot that first day of college. (Seems my claims of being "all grown up" were premature.)

When I hear Rod Stewart's *Wake Up Maggie*, I am 19 again and on my way from my first *very* cool apartment in Boston to my first *very* cool summer job in Boston. I can still remember my brother throwing up on me in the back seat of the car on the way home from a family day trip — and my Dad cleaning up the mess as my Mother wept with laughter in the front seat. And I remember being proposed to over a raw turkey, stuffing spilled everywhere, as if were yesterday.

How ironic that something I call *freeze frames* should warm my heart so completely…

December 23rd, Thursdays, and March

Call me crazy, but I've always thought that December 23rd is the best day of the Christmas season. I've always thought Thursday is the best day of the week. And I've always thought March is the best month of the year. Why? Because I love anticipation — the sheer, childlike joy of looking forward to something wonderful. And the truth is that once you've reached Christmas Eve, Friday, and April, things kind of pick up speed, and the next thing you know, they're over.

It's Christmas morning, and there you sit, knee deep in the mangled remains of your gift-giving efforts — exhausted and broke. Or it's Sunday afternoon, and now that the house is clean, the laundry is done, and the groceries are put away, it's time to get ready for Monday. Or it's early July, and although summer has barely begun, the days are already getting shorter.

Nope. I like December 23rd, Thursdays, and March, because anticipation cannot possibly do battle with reality.

And I do love anticipation...

Thank Goodness

I don't have too many illusions about life, but I'm never ready for events like Aurora, Colorado. Or 9/11. Or Newtown, Connecticut. Or IEDs in Afghanistan. Or suicide bombers anywhere. Or missing children. Or abused animals. Or a lot of other sadnesses.

I'm not sure why that is, the world having long since proven itself to be filled with about as much malevolence as anyone might ever be able to conjure up. But I'm never ready, and whenever something terrible happens, as it seems to every day, my heart always shudders. Then comes the aftermath.

Courageous police or firemen or soldiers race toward perils from which the rest of us flee. Emergency medical personnel respond selflessly with care and compassion. Families and friends and neighbors share support and comfort. Strangers donate and pray and volunteer. And sometimes, the whole world holds its collective breath in sympathy for another soul in pain. That's when I remember just how benevolent people can be.

I am thankful for such goodness…

Congratulations are in Order

A recent trip to the shoe store has revealed that I have achieved something few people achieve: My feet are now size 8 3/4. Yes, 8 3/4. Not 9s, which they used to be. And not 8 1/2s, which would be fine. But 8 3/4 — which is smaller than a 9 and larger than an 8 1/2. Know what that means? It means I need to move to a warm climate where I can wear nothing but flip-flops.

Now, I know we change as we age. For example, I know that I no longer need my distance glasses yet cannot function without my readers. And I know that I weigh less and look worse. Indeed, I foresee a day when, were I better endowed, my bosom would likely pose a greater trip-and-fall hazard than a house full of throw rugs. But this shoe thing is a real problem. Seems my only hope is continued shrinkage, which would be fine with me were it not for the fact that my skin is loose enough already.

I don't mind looking older — I just don't want to look like I'm melting...

The Two-Dog Two Step

I'm not much of a dancer. However, this morning, while single-handedly walking our two little dogs on twin 27-foot retractable leashes with a bag of poop swinging from my arm, I noticed two things: a car was coming and the dogs had crossed back and forth enough to snarl those retractable leashes. With just seconds to rein in the hounds — whose most recent amusement is the occasional, and thus totally unpredictable, lunge at moving cars — I discovered that I'm pretty good at a little something called the *Two-Dog Two Step*.

Juggling blue and red handles with awe-inspiring ease, I swiftly untangled their leads. Then, to get us all to one side of the street together, I performed an astounding pirouette, during which that entire bag of poop flew gracefully over my head without releasing so much as a pellet.

Think anyone was impressed? Nope. The guy in the car had no idea at all what I was doing. And the dogs couldn't have cared less.

Their thing is chasing cars...

The Wicked Witch of the Yard

Last week, in anticipation of Halloween, our next-door neighbors hung a witch in the tree between our two houses. And not just some dopey craft-store witch, you understand. No. They hung a witch that is both life-like and life-sized — which would be great were it not for my dogs, who immediately spotted this new interloper spinning wildly in the breeze and have not stopped barking since.

Yes. I did take them over, hoping that a good sniff might prove to them that she wasn't real. But apparently "real" does not actually have a smell. In fact, having gotten close enough to see that she's big enough to be real, ugly enough to be real, and animated enough to be real, she's real enough to require their ongoing surveillance — and commentary.

And so, I'd like to offer a quick shout out to my neighbors for making this Halloween such wicked fun! You guys owe me a candy bar.

And it had better not be one of those miniature ones…

It's Official. I'm Invisible.

I started thinking I might be when I was waiting in line at the local drugstore, the cashier yelled "I'll take the next customer," and the guy behind me bolted for her counter. And soon after, while shopping at Marshall's, I squeezed back into the rack behind me to let another shopper pass — only to have her park her cart right in front of me and start browsing, leaving me buried in extra-large sweaters.

But I really became suspicious the day I was at a stop sign, brake lights on and blinkers flashing, only to have a lady following well behind me plow full speed into my car. "I didn't see you," said she, her hands on hips in obvious distress that I'd had the nerve to materialize just in time to total her car.

"Listen," said my husband, "people can be rude and people can get distracted. It happens." But that's not it. I really think I've become invisible — and actually, I'm kind of relieved.

Now I can give up dieting...

One Soldier, Immeasurable Thanks.

I have a special place in my heart for soldiers. My Dad served in the Army, and although he was never in combat, he did spend a year away from his family helping to rebuild post-war Japan. Then there's my nephew James, an incredibly brave young man who not only volunteered for the Marines but was deployed twice to Afghanistan. I'm telling you all that because yesterday, when I was grocery shopping for Memorial Day weekend, I saw a young man walking with a limp. Then I noticed he had lost an arm. Never one to be shy, over I went.

"Are you a solider?" I asked, placing one hand softly on his shoulder. "Yes, ma'am," he said, standing just a bit taller. "And you've been wounded," I said. "Yes, ma'am," he repeated. "In Iraq."

Well, my throat closed over, and I could feel my eyes fill with tears for what he had endured — and *would* endure. "I am so sorry," I said. "But I sincerely thank you for your service." "No problem," he replied — which stopped me cold.

"No problem?" I said, gently rubbing that one strong shoulder, as we both smiled sadly at the courage of such understatement. "You really *are* something." But what I wanted to say was this: "I wonder if we Americans are really deserving of such sacrifice" — because I *do* wonder.

Are we really worthy? Do we make a point of knowing what our soldiers are fighting for — and why? Do we read and listen and worry and pray? Do we fly our flags, attend parades, and accord our brave veterans the lifelong honor and care they have earned a thousand times over. Do we spend just a little time each day protecting the freedoms we enjoy here at home in this amazing country as fiercely as we should — freedoms so many, many young soldiers have given both body and soul to defend these past 237 years? Are we grateful enough — and is that even possible?

I think not…

A Little Must is a Big Must

Down in our very dry basement is one corner that smells a bit musty, and I have to be honest, I love it. I love it because it reminds me of what the family cottage smelled like in early summer when we opened up the old place — and I loved that cottage.

One whiff and I'm back on the screened-in porch waiting for the early morning fog to burn off. I'm curled up on chintz-covered furniture so worn that sneakered feet are no longer a threat, playing checkers with my brother. I'm savoring my Dad's homemade clam chowder or watching the grown-ups struggle to hear a Yankees game on the old AM radio. I'm listening to the creaks of floorboards nailed in place by my grandfather so many years before. And I'm falling asleep to sound of waves breaking somewhere off in the darkness.

My husband always said I was a cheap date, and I guess this proves it. A little mildew and I'm not only on vacation but young again!

How great is that — and how lucky is he...

Jergen's Law

I try not to put too much stock in the power of Murphy's Law, which asserts that if something *can* go wrong, it *will*. It's just too negative. But there *are* certain things you *can* count on.

For example, the second you squeeze a dollop of hand lotion into your hand at a red light, that light *will* turn green. Change from the slow line at the check out counter to another that appears to be moving more quickly, and the customer ahead of you will not only need a price check but have coupons, double coupon coupons, and a question about the total. Assume you won't need an umbrella and it won't simply rain. It will rain cats and dogs at precisely the moment you are midway between your car and wherever you are heading.

The thing is, knowing that certain actions trigger certain consequences can be very helpful. I mean, ever since I got that huge bottle of Jergen's for my car, I not only have softer hands.

I don't spend nearly as much time at red lights…

Exclamation Points

I know. I use too many. And believe me, I'm not making excuses, but here's the thing: I write with a level of enthusiasm too hard to convey without them. The trouble is, I'm starting to worry about being perceived as irritatingly effusive, disturbingly chipper — perhaps even (audible gasp) perky, when really, nothing could be further from the truth. I can be very serious. In fact, I can be downright doleful and *still* find a way to work in several dozen.

I remember writing a eulogy once, fully intending to use nothing but periods for optimal *gravitas*. Next thing I knew, there were exclamation points everywhere. I suppose I could have removed a few, but frankly, every last one seemed entirely appropriate. After all, I was honoring a life well lived and a well-lived life merits exclamation points!

In fact, now that I think about just how important living an exclamation-point kind of life really is, I think I might be wrong about using too many! I should probably be using even more!!!

I shall start right now!!!!!!!

I'm Sorry. It Must Be Said.

There is not a single wrinkle cream that really works, and I know that because I have tried them all at least once. And sometimes twice. (As an optimist, I always wonder if I've just gotten a bad batch.) I don't really care, though.

I've earned every laugh line I have thoroughly appreciating both clean and bawdy jokes (especially the bawdy). I've earned every worry line I have, confirming that I am alive and paying attention. And I have earned more than a few other wrinkles from squinting in the sun, enunciating the letter "O", and sleeping on my face — which I have done since birth despite the fact that I have been warned against it by the entire beauty industry.

Besides, worrying about the wrinkles I already have will only cause more, so I don't. Instead, I laugh as much as I want, worry when necessary, squint freely, stress my "O's," and I sleep face down. And I've also invested in plenty of 25-watt light bulbs.

They are much more effective than any wrinkle cream could ever hope to be — and at a fraction of the price...

Sometimes I Wonder

How do I know that what I see as blue is the same as what someone else sees as blue — or if we just learned the word *blue* for two completely different colors? Why do smokers seem to think that the cigarette butts, empty packs, and defunct lighters they throw on the ground are not litter? And what makes anyone think spitting is OK ever anywhere, because it's not. (And if you say *it's not* really quickly, you'll get my point.)

I wonder how squirrels can eat upside down. I would like to know why the average shopper looking for a particular item on a grocery store shelf always seems to lose both peripheral vision and hearing simultaneously while doing so, forcing other shoppers to shout "excuse me" just to get by. I'm curious as to why an awful lot of people think spandex hides fat when it so clearly does not. And I want to know why flies can find their way *into* my house but not back out no matter how many doors or windows I leave open — or how much encouragement I offer.

Finally, I'd really like to know why I am always coming up with weird questions. My husband has assured me that I'm not odd, just very, very observant, which is sweet — but how deluded is he?

I mean, he's seen me talking to those flies…

I Am Becoming My Mother

I am. And the older I get, the greater the similarities — which is not a bad thing, you understand. She was smart and funny and she had a very good heart. But it *is* a little startling.

I mean, she always had something to say about everything, which is clearly a trait of mine. But recently, I discovered that I also have my mother's hands, right down to a couple of age spots she used to complain about. And when I laugh, which I do often and loudly, I hear her. Then last week, I went to the library, and out I came with three fat novels cradled in my elbow and absolute joy in my heart at the thought of all the good reading ahead — just like my mother, who used to visit the library every single week, always taking out three or four books, always stacking them neatly by her chair, and always smiling at the thought of enjoying each in its turn.

"Well, that's that." I said to myself. "I'm becoming Mom" — a turn of events she would have found wildly amusing. I was, after all, the daughter who, in the full ignorance of youth, confused being contrary with being cool.

And you know, at that very moment, I heard this really familiar laughter…

Winter Blossoms

Loving spring and summer as much as I do, it's no wonder that seeing my garden covered with piles and piles of snow makes me antsy for the first warm days in March, when tiny green envoys poke their heads up through newly thawed soil to see if it's safe to get growing. I have a trick, though.

Each week, I make sure I have enough grocery store coupons to save what I need to save on food so that I can treat myself to a small bouquet of daisies. Nothing fancy. No Baby's Breath or bows. Just a dozen fresh daisies.

Once at home on the table in my den, they remind me that somewhere out there it is warm, somewhere out there leaves are green — and just outside my window, beneath vast white drifts, my own little daisies are getting the rest they need for their turn on that table in my den! Gets me through.

Well, that and cheap red wine…

Going Topless

Yup. That was the plan when I bought my cute little convertible a while back. But then came certain revelations — like the fact that putting the top down means going without any real heat or air conditioning and the fact that wind and hair do not mix. But the kicker was discovering that when the top is down, it's not a good idea to be belting out oldies-but-goodies along with the radio (which I do), so that was that. Well, almost.

I did put it down once on the way home from a Moody Blues concert. My husband and I froze, of course — and it took a full hour to comb the snarls out of our hair. But waiting at a stop light, my husband took my hand, and, with the stars shining above and the evening's music still kindling a certain ardor, said softly, "I can smell stuff baking at that Dunkin Donuts over there." "Me, too," I said, breathing deeply.

And you know, for that one very special moment, being topless was bliss…

It's a Wrap

Eventually, Christmas presents must be wrapped. And since the sooner that task is done, the sooner one can settle in and actually start *enjoying* the holiday, I pick a day, light up the tree, put on some carols, clear off the dining room table, and start.

Well, 'round about gift number six, chaos takes over. Sheets of paper, discarded due to miscalculations in box-to-paper estimations, litter the table. Ribbon becomes inextricably tangled. The scissors go missing. Tags don't stick. And pens won't write. Still (and this could be it's own little holiday miracle) that empty circle beneath the tree slowly fills up with brightly wrapped gifts and Christmas is ready. Usually.

One year, our puppy — a good little boy who fancied himself in charge of everything — sniffed all the gifts, then proceeded to hop the entire circumference of that tree on three legs in a misguided effort to both bless and protect every last package. Well, you've never seen so many gifts opened so quickly. It was like Christmas morning on fast forward. But we saved every one, boxes included, and rewrapped the lot — after which I went nose to nose with Mr. Piddles. And what did I say?

"If you ever do that again (wait for it), urine trouble..."

I Could be a Winner

Yes I could! At least that's what the website said when I entered a well-known national sweepstakes last June. But ever since that first entry, I've been stalked by that website, receiving one, two, and sometimes three emails a day warning me that if I don't hit the "continue" button immediately, view a bunch of crummy offers from their prize partners (not that I need to purchase anything to qualify, you understand), and resubmit the same entry I've already submitted several times a day for months, I will forfeit not only my million dollar prize but my $5,000 a week for life. I tell you I am exhausted.

I should have just entered once and been done with it. I should have deleted all those annoying emails. I should have put silly daydreams of that guy and his film crew showing up at my door with a bunch of balloons and an oversized check right out of my head. And I should have found far more constructive ways to use my time. After all the odds of winning are astronomical. And you know, I would have, too, except for one thing.

I could be a winner…

Junk Drawers, Poltergeists, and Other Rationalizations

Every kitchen has a junk drawer. Usually, it's that really skinny one that's not good for much else. So I've been thinking. If everyone has a kitchen junk drawer, as I believe everyone does, is everyone experiencing the same junk drawer phenomenon I am?

Every few months, my junk drawer gets jammed. Some persuasion with a long-handled spoon usually does the trick, at which point I clean it out, leaving behind only the hammer and screwdriver, some glue, a roll of painter's tape, the scissors, and some string — but three or four months later, it jams all over again, and when I finally get it open, I find a massive tangle of junk mixed with some stray crumbs and the occasional withered baby carrot.

Well, *I* certainly don't make that mess. And no one else seems to either. So it has to be poltergeists. It may even be the *same* poltergeists that hide my keys and move my glasses.

Now, I'm wondering about the mess in the garage…

Cell Phones, Darwin, and a Thing Called eVolution

Technology is great. And believe me, I do love my computer. But I do *not* have a fancy cell phone, because there is nothing that could possible happen in Washington or the Kardashian family that I need to know about instantly. And I do *not* carry the one I have except on road trips — or during power outages, when those digital services we insist on bundling crash all at once. But those aren't the only reasons I steer clear of being tethered to the Internet.

I steer clear of being tethered to the Internet because thumbs are getting bigger. Not everyone's thumbs — just those belonging to the people who text and tweet all day. Worse still, their eyes are starting to move independently, too. Oh sure, they appear to be paying attention, but the truth is they've got one eye on you and the other on that gizmo in their hands. And I mean literally.

I suppose such changes are natural — some sort of 21st century accommodation to technology that will come to be known as *eVolution*. In fact, the ability to look both ways before crossing the street *without* having to turn one's head will probably be useful. But it's worrisome – indeed, something to keep an eye on.

I'm just not sure which one…

DNDIY

You know all those great do-it-yourself projects on Do It Yourself TV? Well, *don't*. They look easy. They sound easy. And yeah, the results are always amazing. But none of those projects is really a husband and wife proposition.

Behind those cameras are master carpenters, plumbers, electricians, flooring experts, professional painters, and at least three decorators duking it out over whether to go with eggshell white, natural white, or off white. So when the urge to redo anything more than the kitchen curtains hits you, do not do it yourself. Call someone. Just don't call me and my husband.

Having finally (and not one moment too soon) achieved a kind of Dalai-Lama-level awareness of our limitations, we not only got rid of our DIY aspiration but our tools. Well, most of them. We kept one small hammer and a multi-headed screwdriver for emergency repairs to the projects undertaken before our great awakening. Oh, and there's a bottle of Elmer's in the bathroom, necessitated by my brief love affair with wallpapering.

It's next to the aspirin...

Sometimes, Default is our Own

My grandfather had an interesting way of announcing that dinner was served. He'd say, "Come and get it or I'll give it to the pigs." Of course, he grew up on a farm, making the inelegance of that invitation somewhat colorful. But I've since come to realize that there was more wisdom in his words than he intended! Just think about it!

Life really *is* a big meal — but if you don't grab yourself a plate and dig in as soon as it's ready, yours will consist of nothing more than what's left to all dawdlers: the always-dreaded jello mold, something beige in rapidly congealing cream sauce, limp vegetables, and one very stale roll.

Not that all of what we get out of life is a self-serve proposition. Genetics, environment, and destiny all play a part — as do learning to spell, flossing, and using your blinker. But life is also about choices, and if we don't make them, they are made by default. So when life hollers "come and get it," go!

It's either that or go hungry...

Life After Death

Lots of people don't like cemeteries, but I do. I started liking them a long time ago, when I began helping my Mom plant flowers at our two family plots — and now that it's my turn to tend these tiny gardens, I take great joy in honoring the memory of those who've gone on with mums in the fall, greens at Christmas, pansies at Easter, and a vivid mix of red and pink geraniums each summer. But the truth is, I've learned something from those solitary visits.

One day, while weeding, I looked over to see a doe and her fawn munching the boxwoods on either side of my family's monument. I suppose I should have shooed them away, but suspecting that the departed would much prefer a visit from such gentle creatures to perfectly shaped shrubs, I let them feed. And I do the same for the squirrels and chipmunks and rabbits who dig and dine, often right in front of me, because a little company in such a place is more than simply a welcome surprise.

It's a lovely reminder of that there *is* life after death — in so many ways...

Twelve Days of Tinsel

My parents loved Christmas. Not only did Mom make the whole house twinkle but she made a Santa Claus cookie so beautiful it was more fine art than food. And Dad's passion was the tree.

He'd spend hours choosing it — then hours more moving branches cut from the back into little holes he'd drilled in the front. (No. I am not kidding.) Once sure that his tree was flawless, he'd string the lights, placing each strand as carefully as if he were handling explosives. Then we'd all hang ornaments — small ones at the top, medium ones in the middle, big ones on the bottom — and from that point on, Dad would spend every spare moment hanging tinsel one piece at a time on one branch at a time until he either ran out of tinsel or he ran out of Christmas!

My parents are gone now — and with them went those Santa Claus cookies and all twelve days of tinsel. But I still have their ornaments, and I still hang the small ones at the top, medium ones in the middle, and big ones on the bottom. Hey. Old habits die hard.

So do sweet memories...

Talking Tees

Seems everyone's got something to say these days. And it isn't just people who talk too much. T-shirts are getting downright noisy — and more than a little salty, to boot!

I mean, correct me if I'm wrong, but isn't there something ludicrous — maybe even kind of creepy — about a woman well into her AARP eligibility years wearing a top that says "Want some?" or "Text me at IMHOT?" And those are just the clean ones! There are some that make you wish the illiteracy rate were even higher than it is!

I mean, if clothing manufacturers insist on printing stuff on every t-shirt they make, then I think the very least they can do is provide some age-appropriate options. For example, I might consider wearing a t-shirt that says, "Now looking for my car…" just in case I am. I do like the one that says, "Age improves with wine," because it does. I will even admit to having seriously considered buying the t-shirt that declared, "I may be old, but I got to see all the cool bands" — since I am and I did! But here's the one I would absolutely buy: a custom t-shirt silk-screened with all my personal PIN numbers and passwords – upside down of course, for easy reference. In fact, I'd buy two.

My memory isn't the only thing prone to fading…

Do Not Call

Recently, having triggered a feeding frenzy of telemarketing calls by moving and changing phone numbers, I went to the national *Do Not Call* registry and registered. Since then, the calls have increased — so much so that I think some enterprising telemarketer set up a dummy *Do Not Call* site and is selling those numbers to other telemarketers desperate enough to call anyone anytime anyplace on the off chance of selling something to someone somewhere.

Now, I don't fault the sales people. They're just trying to make a buck. But the calls always come in when I'm midway between the stove and sink — strainer in one hand, pot of boiling whatever in the other. And when I finally pick up, there's always a long, aggravating pause while the computer doing the dialing alerts some sales rep who's off getting coffee that there's a live one on the line. By the time I get back to that strainer in the sink, the only thing steaming is *me*. (Hey. They're not referred to as "cold calls" for nothing.)

So why do I answer? I answer so that I can tell one telemarketing company at a time to "please…take my number off your list." It's slow going, I'll admit — but I can't go to that national *Do Not Call* registry again.

If I do, I may never enjoy a hot meal again…

My Food Channel Moment

I am not a great cook. I am not even all that *willing* a cook, avoiding any recipe having more than four ingredients (and I consider bowls and pans to be ingredients). So when I get excited about a cooking tip, it's got to be big. And this is big. *Really big*. Ready?

Get yourself some corn on the cob. Cut off the fat end, husk and all, about an inch into the bottom of the ear itself. Throw a few into the microwave. Zap them for precisely eight minutes on high. Take them out. Then — and this is the cool part — grab the skinny end and squeeze until the corn pops out, cooked to perfection and totally free of silk. Awesome, huh?

Now, I'll have to admit that I didn't think there could possibly be a single kernel of truth to a no-prep, one-step cooking claim of this magnitude. I mean, really. No husking? No boiling? Yeah, sure. But I've tried it twice — and twice it has worked. In fact, it works so well that I've decided to eat nothing but corn all summer, making me the first official *cornivore* in recorded history!

I shall celebrate by flossing…

Tricky Treats

I dread Halloween. Love the kids and their costumes. Love the pumpkins. Love remembering the anticipation as the sun begins to set and a night of doorbells and giggles begins to unfold. Hate, hate, *hate* the weeks before hand!

I buy a giant bag of candy, and within hours I can hear it calling to me. So I pop a little hole in one corner and remove one miniature chocolate bar. A week later, the bag is empty, the rest of those miniature chocolate bars having somehow escaped through that tiny hole behind closed cabinet doors. I buy another, and the same thing happens — so the day before Halloween, I buy two more bags, just in case, which usually leaves a whole bag of leftover sweets the day after, and they, too, disappear. Drives me crazy.

And that's not the only reason I dread Halloween. It's the unexplained weight gain.

That mystifies me even more than all those missing candy bars....

Spandex

I find that word almost as unattractive as the material — which, in my opinion, is the textile equivalent of spray paint. I mean, let's face it, if you have two ounces of pudge (and all but the youngest among us do), spandex is not your friend. It's like a neon motel sign, which, instead of flashing *Vacancy*, flashes *Full-To-Overflowing*. And that's not the worst part.

The worst part is that they don't seem to manufacture clothes without it anymore — well, except for that baby-doll style that makes everyone look pregnant, and I don't dare wear that for fear that the shock would kill my husband. As a result, my wardrobe is dwindling — and may I add that *dwindling* is a euphemism. Fact is, if you see some poor woman out and about in nothing but a really long t-shirt and mismatched knee-highs, it's probably me.

Try not to stare...

Many Happy Returns

For a long time now I've been keenly aware that most of the things I *really, really* want to buy aren't things I *really, really* want to own. In fact, it's only a matter of actually getting them home before they go from I've-got-to-have-it status into the what-the-hell-was-I-thinking column — at which point I return them and their sales slips to their bags and hang them on the kitchen door so I can take them back as soon as possible and buy something else.

I can't tell you how much this pleases my husband, who considers himself lucky to be married to a woman who has mastered the very fine art of enjoying some good-for-the-soul impulse shopping — then undoing it all a day or two later! He calls these returns "rollovers" on the theory that I've been rolling over the same $29.99 for almost thirty years now. I guess I have to agree.

But secretly, I think of them as a series of birthday gifts to myself — with many happy returns...

Spring Songs and Blue Toes

One of my favorite parts of Spring is that first mild night when the peepers start peeping — and since we have some boggy fields nearby that are home to these tiny creatures, the minute they start singing, I can hear them. It stirs some part of my soul that just can't seem to reawaken without their little chorus — and it also makes me want to open all the windows, clean house, plant something, and put on my flip-flops.

The trouble is, Mother Nature is never in nearly as much of a hurry as I am, so I have to pace myself, cracking windows only slightly, cleaning only a bit more zealously, and letting tulips and daffodils sold in the store sustain me for a few more weeks. But my flip-flops can't wait.

I don them at the first possible chance — and I keep them on regardless of the how cold it might still be.

I simply wear the blue plaid pair so they match my frozen toes...

Nine Eleven

The irony of that date — 911 being the emergency number — may or may not have been a coincidence. All I know is that I remember that day as thousands of dreadful emergencies all happening at once, with precious few rescues.

I'm not sure I have a right to talk about any of it, having been nothing more than an onlooker to the tragedies unfolding. But I will never forget how deeply horrified I was for those so inexorably trapped in the World Trade Centers — and the strange but profound sense I had as each Tower fell that it might have been God bringing them down in the only effective act of mercy still possible.

I know that may seem unforgivably irreverent or wildly childish, but I recall praying that, in the face of such overwhelming suffering, He simply said, "There is no choice. Come with me." And in my mind's eye, as those Towers came down, thousands of souls went up into the bluest of September skies, released from unspeakable agonies into the peace of eternity. It's what I hoped, anyway.

I still do…

In Gratitude for Weeds

My husband and I aren't lawn people — but not because we don't appreciate a beautiful lawn. We do. We just can't *have* one.

With two dogs and a well, pesticides and herbicides are out, and we've long since given up on the theory that good grass crowds out weeds, because it doesn't. We top seed the bare areas every year, we lime and fertilize appropriately, but by mid-July, our yard boasts exactly 36 blades of magnificent Kentucky Blue mixed with crab grass, clover, wild violets, and some kind of creeping thing that fills in where the rest leave off.

The thing is, it's green. Very green. A deep, rich green unaffected by days without rain and withering hot sun. In fact, while all the beautiful lawns are losing their battle with the elements, our field of weeds thrives, thick and lush. It's a thing to behold, really — as long as we squint. So squint, we do, from mid-July on.

And you know what else? The money we save is green, too. Very green! A deep, rich green!

I think we're onto something...

Lighten Up

Well, that's it. The holidays are officially over. My beautiful tree is gone, its lights and ornaments tucked safely away in soft beds of white tissue paper — and frankly, I am having warm-glow withdrawal.

My kitchen lacks the wondrousness it had achieved just days before Christmas, when the makings of a splendid family dinner filled the fridge, and small plates of cookies and chocolates tied with love and ribbons for friends and neighbors lined the counters just waiting to be delivered. Even the dogs, who do not fully understand all the fuss, are aware that their prospects for yet another haul of squeaky toys and chicken-wrapped sweet potatoes is not good.

And so, as the reds and greens and silvers and golds of December yield to the blues of January, I try to stay focused on the one redeeming fact that helps me to lighten up a little: The days are now getting longer! And while there are some cold, gray stretches to come, not to mention snow and sleet, followed by rain and mud, April is out there. It is!

Until then, I'll be in here…

Saved by the Nut with the Dogs

There are those who would argue that the very essence of tragedy is its scope, but I believe that small lives endure small tragedies, too — like earthworms.

I thought a lot about that when I was walking with my dogs the other day. It was barely an hour after another summer downpour, yet the sun had already turned the sidewalks into a skillet, leaving worms by the score sizzling halfway across the blistering concrete. Some were simply too dried up to help, but others could be saved, so I picked them up and placed them one after the other in the grass, hoping they would burrow deep into the cool, healing soil as quickly as possible. I'm not sure the survivors understood their good fortune, but it doesn't really matter. No living creature is too small to benefit from a little kindness. More importantly, no living creature is too great to offer it.

Of course, my neighbors think I'm nuts. I think the dogs might, too. But that's OK. Somewhere out there is a worm who made it home that night and is still telling all his buddies about the nut with the dogs.

I like that…

I Do Not Love Valentine's Day

It can be much too stressful. I mean, as a kid I worried about getting as many flimsy paper cards as everyone else. In high school I obsessed over whether or not my boyfriend would sign his card *Love, So-and-So* — and, if he did, what that might mean. And when I finally had a husband to send over-priced roses declaring me his one and only (as if marrying me didn't count), I was sure my worries were over — only to discover I was wrong. Very, very wrong.

The truth is, we struggled to close the gap between my head-in-the-clouds expectations and his feet-on-the-ground practicality until the day it finally hit me: Grand gestures aren't nearly as important as the little everyday ones — you know, that hug for no reason…the unexpected favor…those little private jokes that no one else gets.

So this Valentine's Day, the stress is gone — finally. I know I'm loved. Also, I have convinced Mr. Practicality that chocolate is an actual food group.

Guess I'm pretty much good to go…

Dog People

Actually, there's no such thing. And I know that because I was a dog person — right up until a little cat named *Whispers* came along.

Abandoned not once but twice, he had actually lived in the home we'd just bought. So when the neighbors, who'd kinda/sorta been caring for him, asked if we would watch him Thanksgiving weekend — and did so Thanksgiving morning with their bags packed and motor running, I agreed. And around dusk, in he came, heading straight to the basement.

Curious, I followed him down, only to find him curled tightly into himself on a totally empty shelf, grateful for nothing more than the warmth and familiarity of that crummy spot. Well, that was that. I quickly made him a soft bed in a cozy moving box. And by the next afternoon, our guest room — along with a proper bed, real feeding bowls, toys and treats, some primo catnip, 24/7 maid service, and my heart — were his.

Whispers left us last year. But for the last eight of his 16 years, he had the best life two humans and a couple of goofy dogs could give him. And I know that because whenever we four went for a walk, he'd join us, proudly proclaiming, "I have a family again! Yes, I do!"

Maybe he was lucky, but we were luckier...

Let's Get Real

Reality TV isn't really real. It's just really scripted — including that show in which house-hunting couples stand in the middle of a brand new high-end kitchen with granite countertops, cherry cabinets, and stainless steel appliances and say "this isn't really our style." (*This isn't really our style?* Who says that in the middle of an $80,000 kitchen?) I say that if reality TV wants to get real, they should plant a single camera in the home of any not-so-handy couple deluded enough to undertake a home improvement together — like mine.

We hung some mini-blinds on the screened-in porch last weekend because (and these are what are known as *famous last words*) "how hard could it be?" Well, my husband, who measures 30 times and cuts once, took an hour and a half to install mini-blind number one. So I, who have no patience (or standards) suggested he eat lunch — then hung the remaining three in just under an hour.

Needless to say, these divergent styles generated a rather colorful (and apparently loud) dialogue that was completely unscripted and arguably worthy of primetime. That's what the neighbors tell us, anyway.

At least, the ones still willing to make eye contact…

Grid and Bear It

I know someone whose goal is to live *off the grid*, using no utilities at all. Well, frankly, I thought that was kind of nuts. Then came our autumn nor'easter, delivering a foot of wet snow to trees still sporting their leaves, and within hours, it wasn't the leaves falling but the trees — and with them, the grid itself.

Well, there was all kinds of hand wringing and finger pointing, yet days later, the grid was still on the ground — and sadly, having not prepared for all of the wood-chopping, fire-stoking, goat-milking, chicken-raising kinds of activities one must master to live without that grid, all that was left was to sit, awaiting its return, and with it the warm rooms, hot showers, ringing phones, whirring computers, working stoves, and flushing toilets we all take for granted. A little wiser, though still not able to raise chickens or chop wood, we're looking into buying a generator.

And may I say that if there is even one dollar left after that purchase, we're spending it on stock in that generator company…

Hard-Wired Memories

With winter now here, there is a stretch of road I travel where the sun, low in the sky but still very strong, glares on-and-off so sharply and erratically through trees empty of leaves that it reminds me of the strobe lights popular in the '70s. Unfortunately, that, in turn, reminds me of the night I discovered that under those strobes fed by black lights, one and only one of my 28 teeth — a crowned front tooth — would fluoresce a dreadful bluish white.

Now, that appalling discovery wouldn't have been so bad had I made it early in the evening, when I could have smiled a little less. But no! I grinned my brains out all night long, one lone tooth glowing wildly like a witch's fang. It still makes me shudder — and it also makes me wonder why memories like that are so hard-wired into my brain while all the really good ones are so much more fleeting. Memories like how great I looked in a mini-skirt. Or so I thought. I *was* a little chunky.

Uh oh…

Hmmmmmmm...

Recently, I came home to a message that an old friend who was in town visiting her parents had called. "Here's her folks' number," said my husband. But I didn't need it. I returned that call as if it were 1965 because the number was still in my head — along with the numbers of all my other childhood friends, the correct time, two AM stations I used to listen to on my transistor radio, an old boyfriend, and the office from which my Dad retired 34 years ago. That's when it occurred to me that I was in trouble.

I mean, with my digital phone capturing and storing all of that information for me, I don't know *anyone's* number anymore, which means that the expression *use it or lose it* isn't an exaggeration. In fact, it's anything but, so let's just hope I never lose that phone.

If I do, the only calls I'll be able to make will be for the correct time or to dedicate a song on WDRC...

How to Live to be 100

That was the title of the article — and the photo selected to accompany the article was of someone eating cereal. Well, my first reaction was "Oh, come on…it can not be that easy," so I read the whole thing, and, as expected, eating cereal for breakfast is healthy, as long as it's high fiber. But there was more.

The actual *longevity list* included about 20 other things you should do, twice as many that you shouldn't, and by the time I worked out that I was probably not going to make it to dinner — much less 100, my head was pounding.

Well, I'm no fool. Having just finished reading that stress is bad and avoiding it good, I got rid of that article with all its depressing lists — and what a surprise. My headache went with it! Now, with a little luck, I have high hopes of making it to the weekend.

And if I start eating more high fiber cereal, I may even push through to spring…

My Little Bug's Little Bug was Bugging Me a Little

Even the daisies on the dashboard looked worried. So back I went to the dealer, only to discover it wasn't minor, it wasn't normal for a car with such low mileage — and my extended warrantee had ended just five weeks earlier. (That's right. Five.) Well, there was some discussion about all of that, during which I may have been less than gracious. Then Ray, the Service Manager, said "leave it with me." So I did, and one week later he called to tell me that *my* problem was really *their* problem, so they would be happy to take care of it.

That's right! *They* would not only take care of it. They would be *happy* to take care of it. Imagine! And because they did the right thing, I'm doing the "write" thing, too, offering as public a "thank you" as I can manage to a car company that could have told me and my little Bug with the little bug to bug off — but did not. They are very wonderful — with a capital "V" and a capital "W"!

In fact, they've left me speechless, which, as most people already know, does not happen easily —or often…

Birdfeeders, World Peace, And Squirrels.

I bought a birdfeeder last week. Two days later, it was on the ground in six pieces — the birdseed gone. Undaunted, I bought a sturdier model, which seemed to draw an even wider variety of birds, along with squirrels and chipmunks — all of which dined in such splendid harmony that I wondered aloud why we humans can't be more like them. Then the hostilities began.

One squirrel, unhappy with his share of the meal, took a wild dive, landing atop the feeder and swinging it 'round until it was nearly empty. Then he and his buddies dug in, chasing away morning doves and sparrows, sending the chipmunks scrambling for cover in the bushes — and generally providing a pretty good explanation of what happened to the first bird feeder, as well as no less than fifteen pounds of pricey birdseed.

"We can't continue feeding them," said my husband, mentally calculating what a year's worth of birdseed would probably cost us at the present rate of consumption — and frankly, I didn't know what to say because I adore my critters. But I promised him one thing.

If there's ever a knock on the door, and when I open it, an 85-pound squirrel grumbles, "Hey lady, we need more food out here," that feeder comes down...

Summer Sounds

Something's been missing from my summers, and I think it's the crickets. Oh, they're out there, singing away. But we're in here — windows closed, AC on — so we can't hear them. Makes me think back to when I was a kid and there was no summer night too hot to sleep as long as I could put my pillow by the window and listen to them croon.

And there's another hot-summer-night sound I remember, too.

My Dad, obviously not as soothed by the crickets as I, had traded his soft bed for the cold flagstones on our sun porch to get some relief. Unfortunately, when my Mom went looking for him, there he was, splayed out on the cool stone floor in his boxers, still as a corpse – which is apparently what she thought he had become, because the shriek she let out continues to echo in my mind along with my crickets.

It's just a little louder…

I Give Up

Fresh out of college, I took a job as an English teacher. In fact, I taught writing, which entailed teaching formal English grammar. As a result, I am a truly tortured soul.

I have nightmares over the improper placement of commas and semi-colons; I am driven to aspirin whenever I hear someone say *if I was* instead of *if I were*; and I bristle when I read that something is *comprised of*, since the whole comprises the parts — not the other way 'round.

That said, I know how irritating I am to those not quite so steeped in introductory gerund phrases and the correct use of our language's more arcane words. (See! *Arcane*. Who says that?) And so, I've begun to throw in an errant comma every now and then. I practice using fragments. And I am trying to start as many sentences as I can with the word *but.* Indeed, my writing could soon consist almost entirely of dangling participles because I am nothing if not hip and happenin'!

OK, where's my aspirin…

Leaf Envy

Raking leaves is like digging a hole in water. In fact, after several weekends spent herding leaves to the woods only to find ourselves awash in new arrivals, my husband and I have developed *leaf envy*.

I mean, we look at homes all around ours and can't help but notice that their trees are bare and their yards are raked — the only real vestige of fall a small phalanx of brown bags at the curb. Then there's our house, a house still completely surrounded by trees in all stages of droppage, including one particularly stubborn pear tree determined to hang on to its leaves until January.

We talked about buying a small flamethrower to mount a sort of preemptive strike, but dark images of unintended consequences ended that. Now, we just go out and glare at the trees — especially that pear — willing those leaves to fall.

Hasn't made them drop any faster, but three of our squirrels have moved next door, and I'm pretty sure one of them flipped me the bird...

I've had Qwite a Revelation

If, while typing, one hits both the "q" and the "w" on the keyboard at the same time — which is easy to do since they are side by side, one not only achieves precisely the sound that "qu" is intended to achieve but eliminates one whole keystroke!

Now, there are those who will qwestion — indeed qwibble with — the wisdom of making such a change in spelling, lest we disturb the eqwuilibrium of all English-speaking people, but a fact is a fact. Typing "q" and "w" together is phonetically eqwivalent to typing both "q" and "u" separately (actually better), and it's much qwicker, saving those of us who use a keyboard even qwasi-routinely some seven or eight minutes across the course of our lifetime. And although it's hard to qwantify a thing like that, saving even a few minutes is hard to qwarrel with! And so, I have no qwalms whatsoever about advocating that "qu" be replaced with "qw" at the earliest opportunity.

The sqweamish will simply have to adjust...

Ah, the Wonders of Nature

Remember that old nursery rhyme about the old lady who swallowed a fly, then swallowed a spider to eat the fly, then swallowed a bird to eat the spider, and so on? Well, that's what's been going on here at our new house, except it started with ants. Tiny ants. But ants nonetheless. So I asked our neighbor if he gets ants. "Yeah. Every Spring," he said. "But don't worry. The spiders eat them." And he wasn't kidding.

Soon after, those ants pretty much disappeared — which is when we noticed the spiders. Big, outside spiders. Harmless I'm told — and desperately shy. But let's face it, once you know that big outside spiders know how to become big inside spiders, they might as well be perched on your nose. So back I went to my neighbor. "About those spiders…do they go away?" "Oh, absolutely," he replied. And you know, I should have left it at that. But no. I had to ask. "Does something eat them?" Well, he thought about that for a moment. Then he smiled. "You don't want to know."

The exterminator comes Thursday…

Finally. It is Spring.

And I for one am relieved. I mean, after last winter, when the snow was so deep we looked like rats in a giant white maze, followed by October's not-so-amusing little storm, with its tangle of splintered trees and downed power lines, I was braced for this winter to provide five solid months of cold, wet crud. Instead, everything was so weirdly temperate that we were all tiptoeing around, wary of jinxing such good fortune — and that's when I realized something.

Mother Nature has learned what I learned when I was very young/stupid and thought practical jokes were hilarious: You don't have to actually *do* anything to drive everyone nuts — you just have to make them *think* you did. I got so good at it, that all I had to do was smile and the whole dorm scrambled to check their rooms.

Anyway, that's what happened to us. We prepared and we worried until, certain that having had almost no winter at all, we were really in for it. Then nothing — the meteorological equivalent of my evil little smile. But it's officially Spring now, so we can relax, right?

OK, I'm buying some more ice melt…

Neighbors

We almost moved last summer. In fact, we had all kinds of practical reasons for doing so, but we changed our minds. After all, we love our little house, quirky as it is. And we love the fact that after thirty years of moves, we have finally put down some real roots. One of the most compelling factors, however, was our neighbors.

We don't socialize in any formal way. Mostly, we just visit on the street while our dogs sniff each other. But in addition to long conversations curbside, we exchange favors (like pet sitting) and share riches (like summer-ripened tomatoes and fresh-cut zinnias) — so last week, when I was out shoveling, I wasn't surprised to hear my next-door neighbor fire up his snow blower and head my way. "Thought you could use a hand," he said.

Imagine trading such kindness for one extra bathroom…

Just Say Whoa!

They say that when the going gets tough, the tough get going, and I think that's probably true — except when the going involves shopping. I mean, when my husband and I realized that the economy was toast, we slammed the brakes on all non-essential spending by *not* going shopping unless absolutely necessary. And when that didn't do it, we upped the ante even more, agreeing to *not* go into a checkout line anywhere with anything *ever* until we'd had time to think that purchase to death.

Well, that did it! You would not believe the savings! But the truth is that frugality had nothing to do with it. Seems that when you reach our age, waiting even a few minutes before buying something pretty much means forgetting what it was you were going to buy, making our shopping "whoas" the perfect solution to our budget woes.

Hey. Works for us...

Lefty Loosey, Righty Tighty.

I know. Life isn't predictable. If it were, none of us would ever get caught in traffic. We'd have an umbrella whenever we need it. All size 8 shoes would fit all size 8 feet. Housebreaking a puppy would be easy. There would be no divorces. And the box that my hair color comes in wouldn't say "results may vary" in disturbingly large letters. But the old *lefty loosey, righty tighty* rule had always been something I could count on — my North Star, steadfast and true. (Well, whenever I needed to unscrew something anyway.) Then last week, while cleaning our outside lights, I discovered something.

I discovered that every single one of our exterior fixtures has tiny little fasteners that tighten to the left, *not the right*, which not only isn't right but will never rhyme. And so, in one fell swoop, the world became totally random — a complete cosmic crapshoot.

On the bright side, life will now be one surprise after another. (Well, whenever I needed to unscrew something anyway.)

Besides, those stupid *lefty tighty, righty-loosey* light fixtures probably won't need cleaning for at least another year…

I Could Be Getting Old

From inside looking out, it doesn't seem as if I am. I feel about 23. Always have for some odd reason. Then there was last week's birthday, and though I won't say what number kept appearing on cards, it was not 23 — so I've developed a plan.

For starters, I'm going to spend more time sitting inside my VW Bug listening to '60s and '70s music. Having spent a lot of time doing precisely that when it actually *was* the '60s and '70s, it always makes me feel younger. This could mean spending some evenings in the garage, but I'm game.

Next, I'm going to avoid cameras, full-length mirrors, shorts, sleeveless tops, bathing suits, and fluorescent lighting for the rest of my life. This could take some doing, but having seen myself in photos, full-length mirrors, shorts, sleeveless tops, bathing suits, and fluorescent lighting, I am resolute.

Finally, I'm going to optimize the more youthful appearance I seem to be acquiring as my eyesight goes by losing my glasses as often as possible — a strategy which is already working quite well with little effort.

True. None of this will turn back the proverbial hands of time. But I said it was a plan.

I didn't say it was a good one…

I Have a Confession to Make

I've demanded more of my teeth than I should have. I've used them to break off stray threads and I've used them to hold stuff when both hands are full. I've used them to rip open cellophane bags that say "tear here" but don't. I've used them to hold one end of a ribbon when I'm tying a bow. And I've used to them to crack open pistachio nuts, start oranges when a knife isn't handy, and chip away the glue that always gets on my fingertips no matter how careful I am (and which always dries instantly on everything except the thing I am gluing). I've even used them to steady a favorite bracelet whenever I hook or unhook the clasp. Frankly, it's amazing that I haven't broken any, given all that I have asked — indeed, implored them to do in moments of quiet desperation. (OK, impatience.)

So from this point forward, I will beg no more, regardless of how great the need, regardless of how dire the circumstance. It won't be easy, but I am committed to protecting my teeth, because you know what they say.

Beggars can't be chewers...

My Tree. My Roots.

I do love Christmas, and maybe that's part of why I look forward to putting up my Christmas tree. But the truth is, I look forward to putting up my Christmas tree because its branches hold more than decorations. They hold my memories.

All of the handcrafted trimmings were made by someone I knew, someone I loved. All of the little figurines arrived as gifts, carefully chosen for me by family or friends. And all of the glass ornaments, chipped and crazed as their paint might be, take me back to a time when my parents handed them to us kids one at time, reminding us to be very careful lest we drop and break one. Even the rusty old hooks still dangling from their tops — hooks that were once as bright and shiny as childhood itself — are important to me, because they were placed on those ornaments by a mother and father long missed.

And so, when my tree goes up, so do my spirits. Because it isn't just a tree.

It's my roots...

Led Zeppelin: Now Appearing in Baked Goods

Last week, while prowling through fresh produce at the grocery store, I noticed that a Beatles tune was playing on the store's PA system — and by the time I rounded the bend into snack foods, it was Mick Jagger and *Goodbye Ruby Tuesday*.

Well, anxious as I was to finish up and get home, I found myself slowing down somewhere between pet supplies and toiletries to enjoy a little Crosby, Stills, and Nash...some vintage Clapton...an early favorite by Janis Joplin...and an old Air Supply hit. And when I finally did get to the check out counter, I was actually singing — which is when it occurred to me that if the music of my youth is now the Muzak of my supermarket, then life is destined to become one long rock concert, minus some of the bass and most of the decibels.

Well, I think that's awesome! I mean, it actually makes me look forward to grocery shopping. I just wish they took requests.

A little Jimi Hendrix in the deli section would be cool...

Things are Not Looking Up at Downton Abbey

OK. I know it's just a TV show. But I had really high hopes during last night's season finale, when I counted three blossoming romances — the cook and her grocer, Branston and that pushy maid, and the senior Mrs. Crawley and *everyone's* family doctor — only to watch all three fizzle like one of Ethel's kidney soufflés.

And yeah, I know it's just a TV show. But Edith is about to step in it with her editor— and really. Hasn't she been through enough?

And yes, it *is* just a TV show. But it sure looked like Mary and Matthew were going to fade into the credits, happy at the birth of their new as-yet-to-be-named son. But no. We were left with the image of Matthew lying dead while Mary coos adoringly at her now fatherless child.

I just hope the scriptwriters understand what a mess they've made of everyone's life — characters and viewers alike. It's just not right. And as far as I'm concerned, the only way to make it up to us will be to have Carson and Mrs. Hughes get drunk and elope, with the Dowager Countess driving the car.

Ok. You're right. It's just a TV show. And I know that. I do.

Kind of…

Hat Hair

Now that we're knee deep in winter — and the snow that's come with it, I feel the need to come right out and say it: I can live with every aspect of this challenging season but hat hair. I simply cannot stand having hat hair.

I mean, unless you're blessed with bounce-back curls or a completely bald head, the kind of hat necessitated by the average New England winter invariably renders the wearer with a headful of flat-as-a-pancake hair which, when combed, floats sideways, snapping and crackling with enough static electricity to power a small transformer. My solution? I don't have one.

Occasionally, I do wear a hood, but only occasionally, since hood hair is almost as nasty as hat hair. Mostly, I just endure — sometimes happily hatless and sometimes haplessly hatless. My husband just shakes his head.

I might, too, if mine weren't frozen...

Paul McCartney Got Married. Again.

And again, there was a twinge. Granted, it wasn't as noticeable as the one I felt when he and Linda tied the knot back in the sixties. That one was serious. After all, the Beatles debuted on Ed Sullivan just as I was entering my teens and disbanded just as I was exiting them, making their songs the musical score of my entire adolescence — and each, in their turn, the focus of my undying affection.

It's not that any one of us besotted schoolgirls really thought we'd meet much less marry a Beatle, but when you're delusional enough to think teased hair and white lipstick looks good, you can imagine almost anything. And so, when Paul McCartney got married that first time, it was tough going…well, for a few days anyway. And when he got married again recently, there was still this tiny little twinge.

Fortunately, I have my own Paul McCartney of more than 30 years. And not only is he very into music. He also calls me Jude.

Be still my heart…

The Good Humor Man

It was just before dinner on one of this summer's hottest days. My husband and I were sitting quietly on the front porch. The dogs were stretched out on the cool stone floor. And the only real sound was the cicadas humming their one-note mantra. Then we heard it. *Turkey in the Straw* played on a toy piano. No. It wasn't heat stroke. It was the Good Humor Man — a rarity these days — and immediately, we remembered.

We remembered racing to the house in search of a parent and the quarters needed to buy something cold and sweet…standing in line with the neighborhood kids until it was our turn to order…then settling down in the shade of a tree to savor what would soon become a drippy mess.

"Good times," I said to my husband. "The best," he responded. And for the next few minutes, we watched and listened and smiled as the Good Humor Man drove from one end of our neighborhood to the other over and over and over — that one passage of *Turkey in the Straw* playing over and over and over. And about the time he made his third pass, the adult in me returned. "You know…" I began. "Yeah?" said my husband, obviously expecting another heart-warming recollection.

"They may call those drivers *Good Humor* men, but fifty bucks says they go mad listening to that music…"

January Means Back to Normal

And as far as I'm concerned, it has come not a moment too soon. I mean, I do love the holidays. But boy, are they ever a challenge.

For one thing, my diet begins to consist almost entirely of sugar, refined flour, more sugar, and several particularly festive artificial food colorings, including Green #3, Red #40, and Brilliant Blue #1 — any one of which could be used as a night light in a pinch.

Then there's my ability to adhere to a budget, which rivals an art form most of the year yet declines in exact proportion to how close we get to Christmas, with most purchases preceded by the words "Hey, what the hell" and followed by the words "Hey, what the hell."

Finally, my penchant for keeping a tidy house pretty much disappears, as energy is redirected into other essential pursuits — like eating holiday cookies and shopping.

So I welcome January — although I do so with heavier thighs, a lighter wallet, and a slightly fershimmeled house!

But then hey, what the hell…

The Walk

When my husband and I moved to a smaller neighborhood a while back, the number of different walks we could take with our puppies was limited. Indeed, the sameness of it all made us long for our old streets. But then we discovered the local dog park — and after that, the miles of trails surrounding that dog park, and now, at long last, we are *home*.

Every day, I take the little ones on *The Walk*, meandering through lush woods obviously suffused with scents of all sorts, given the amount of sniffing that goes on. Racing back and forth, they scan the tall grass, low bushes, and every pebble in between for signs that another four-legger, domestic or wild, has been — and gone, conferring snout to snout over the source of each smell before moving on to the next.

It's a long process, our walk, but I don't mind a bit. Those woods are my church, and while my dogs savor life nose to the ground, I whisper prayers of gratitude to a Divinity so clearly evidenced by the cycle of life, death, and rebirth underway all around us in the rich tangle of young seedlings and lifeless branches, glorious wildflowers, and spent leaves.

I'm just glad my nose isn't as good as theirs or that walk might not be nearly as lovely…

Our Blessed Event

Of course, we *did* notice our new feathered friend the day we opened the front door and she flew into the house. But the truth is that it wasn't until she began dive-bombing us every time we went in or out that we actually caught on: That tiny little spitfire had not only built herself a nest in the flowers on my front door. She had also built herself a family, with four tiny eggs waiting to hatch.

Well, hatch they did — and what a kick we got out of watching Mom fly in and out all day with worms and bugs of increasingly large size for her rapidly growing brood. Then late last week, she delivered a rather formidable insect to her offspring, and we knew time was short. Our babies were ready to fledge.

The porch is very quiet now. And except for the occasional chipmunk dashing back and forth, it's pretty dull, too. But yesterday I spotted a different little bird doing a "dibs" dance on one of my huge Boston Ferns, so with a bit of luck, we'll be ducking and dodging and tiptoeing around again soon! Good thing, too.

This empty nest syndrome is for the birds…

What is it About Jelly Beans?

They're around all year long, albeit in the dark recesses of the candy aisle where I never (OK, seldom) venture, yet I barely give them a thought. Then comes the morning after Valentine's Day, and there they are — bags and bags of these tiny little confections on display everywhere — and I am in trouble.

Oh sure. After a few thousand I do get kind of sick of them, but until I've eaten that few thousand, I can't get enough. Maybe it's fond memories of waking up Easter morning to a house full of them, just waiting to be gathered up into ribboned baskets by sticky little hands. Or maybe it's the fact that they are pure sugar and thus flawless in their complete lack of even one nutritionally redeeming quality. But it doesn't matter.

It has become quite apparent that jelly beans are destined to remain an integral part of my life — and my thighs — forever...

Brain Songs

It seems I have a kind of, well…affliction. My brain contains a small continuous reel tape that makes it possible for me to hear a song, then replay one or two measures of that song over and over in my head until I hear another song catchy enough to take its place.

Two years ago, I had Burl Ives singing *Have a Holly Jolly Christmas* for three solid weeks — and really, I thought I'd go quite mad. But then *Auld Lang Syne* took over on New Year's Eve, followed by a dreadful fifties song called *If I Knew You Was Comin' I'd Have Baked a Cake* shortly thereafter, neither of which was great but both of which were a relief from Burl and his jolly holly.

The good news is that there is an upside to this problem. I don't need an iPod. I don't even need a radio. I am my own irritating amusement.

Saves me a fortune in batteries…

Another Nine Eleven

Every year, the sadness of that day's memories returns — memories which remain as clear as the skies were that beautiful September morning. But this year, I'm sad about other things, too.

In the days and weeks and months following 9/11, you couldn't count the flags, there were so many. Houses of worship overflowed. Strangers hugged. And elected officials spoke with one voice, one allegiance. Now, just over a decade on, things are very different, with Americans divided not only by beliefs but by a growing anger and intolerance for each other's beliefs. What happened to us — to the profound unity born of such unspeakable tragedy? Politics.

Instead of working together toward the salvation of a country hobbled by mounting debt, soaring costs, and dwindling employment, too many politicians at all levels continue to see their own reelection as paramount, settling for slogans instead of solutions and delivering half-truths instead of the hard truths Americans have always, always been brave enough to face. Among friends and families and neighbors and colleagues, there is little real debate, because patience and respect are no longer central to the discourse — only the false notion that while diversity in some forms is sacrosanct, diversity of opinion equals betrayal. And I fear that we ourselves are unraveling the exquisitely woven fabric of our own great nation far more effectively than all the hijacked airliners in the world ever could have, which is a horrible shame.

This is not who we are…

The Holidays are Here!

Let the shopping begin!

OK, I'm done. No, really. I am! For years, I'd try to put my finger on just the right gift for everyone by engaging in an aimless wall-to-wall mall-to-mall wander. Now, I simply put my finger on my laptop mouse — after which magical search engines not only provide what I am looking for but at the best possible price!

Sometimes, I buy online and have it shipped. Sometimes, I just go get it. Either way, I've saved the money I will probably need for food or home heating oil or taxes — and the time I would rather invest in other things. Things like making gingerbread men, who taste a lot better than they look…singing along to Christmas carols with notes I can no longer reach but insist on going for…staring at my tree until it all blurs into a heavenly glow of light and colors and memories…and finally, spending a couple of hours at the local dollar store so I can fill stockings with pure silliness and love.

Oh, and will you look at that!

Here comes Santa — again — in that wonderful brown truck…

Moving

We just finished moving. We thought about doing so last year and backed out. This time — for a lot of what we thought were really great reasons — we forged ahead, but our instincts were right.

Moving is like taking the tidy little bits and pieces of your life and throwing them up into the air directly over a mud puddle. Underwear goes missing. Shoes turn up in roasting pans. And, if I'm not mistaken, I had more than one dog. (Just kidding — but only just!) Most horrifying, however, were the disturbingly large dust bunnies that began appearing not long after the movers arrived to load up.

"Sorry about that," I said to one of the guys, who, straining under the weight of a couch, clearly couldn't have cared less. "I like to think I'm a pretty good housekeeper." "Oh that's nothin'," he replied. "You should have seen the ones behind your bed!"

Note to self: Check mud puddle for self-esteem…

Nature's Grand Finale

Recently, I found myself despairing over what seemed to be a pretty drab fall — the trees in my yard having achieved only some dark golds and maroons not especially inspiring. Then yesterday, I took a different turn on one of my walks.

Well, lined up along one side of the street was a stand of maples the color of lemon, orange, and raspberry sherbet. In fact, they were so bright, they actually glowed in the late afternoon sun, and that's when it occurred to me.

Those trees ablaze with color were like that last burst of fireworks on the Fourth of July or the big finish to a Broadway musical — you know, when the whole cast takes the stage singing and dancing and making you wish you had enough talent to join them. Yup. Those trees were Nature's grand finale — and almost enough to make up for the months of bare limbs and gray skies destined to come. Almost.

It takes an awful lot to make up for February…

Mosquitoes

Want to know when lots and lots of loooooong red lights are a welcome thing? When you need to scratch the arch of your right foot with the big toe of your left foot because a twelve-pound mosquito has managed to bite you there. I did that the other day, and that's when I vowed to find out just what good those flying you-know-whats are to anyone.

Well, apparently mosquito larvae are a significant food source to some fish, while adult mosquitoes are tasty little meals for bats, spiders, and birds. In fact, they are — and I quote — "a biomass of food for wildlife on the lower rungs of the food chain" which if eliminated "would have an enormous adverse affect on the entire ecosystem."

Yeah? Well, I don't know about you, but I'm willing to risk it, because this year's mosquitoes aren't insects. They're like small armies of flying monkeys dispatched by the Wicked Witch of the Swamp — and the horror of each encounter is yet another round of welts that make even the most stalwart among us pray for lots and lots of looooong red lights. The upside?

My new fragrance is "Off" bug spray, which — though a little pungent — is much cheaper than perfume…

My Box of Dirt

Last month, facing both an empty front garden and an equally empty wallet, I bought myself a seed starter box and some seeds. Then I planted them. I even drew a nice little diagram of which flowers would be bursting forth in which section.

Well, I watered that box regularly and fertilized as directed. I made sure it got six hours of sun whenever there was sun to be had. I moved it outside for some fresh air when the days were mild, taking it back in at night to avoid any frost. I even put on my reading glasses every morning to see how things were going — and believe me, those reading glasses were necessary. They still are.

Except for a few tiny seedlings clustered here and there, which I will plant with pride, that seed starter box is mostly just a box of dirt. Am I discouraged? No. OK, yes. But I'm thinking that all of this is a sign — a sign that the Universe wants me to go out and stimulate the economy by buying some perennials that I probably can't afford — but can actually see — at my local garden center. So I'm off to do just that.

I do not argue with the Universe…

American Idle

I have always felt that housework is just about the most thankless job on the face of the earth. I mean, you clean — and within minutes, the decline begins. Crumbs materialize, dust gathers, fuzz bunnies form, grimy fingerprints appear, toothpaste drips, dishes happen, laundry occurs, and waste baskets fill. It's like trying to dig a hole in water.

Then, about a year ago, I watched one episode of a reality show called *Hoarding: Buried Alive*, and I have to say that it was enormously therapeutic. Spending just one hour looking at houses where no one has thrown anything (and I do mean anything) away for years, let alone dusted, put things in serious perspective. So now I watch it every week — and it's a miracle, really. The more I watch, the better my house looks, all from the comfort of my couch!

Oh sure. I still clean. But during that one hour, I really do feel more inclined to throw in the dishtowel and relax. Indeed, during that one hour, I am the star of my own little reality series.

I call it "American Idle…"

The Real Flower Power

The other day I had one of those moments I love. Walking across a very hot, dry parking lot on a very hot, dry day, I spotted a small pink flower growing up from between the cracks in the pavement, smiling bravely — joyously — into the afternoon sun. Imagine such a thing.

Against all odds, this delicate little sprout staked its claim to a gritty sliver of earth and made do, pushing its way through worthless sand and some old cigarette butts toward the light to blossom. And at the risk of getting too deep in the existential weeds, it made me wonder why all of us can't do the same — why all of us *don't* do the same.

I mean, as blessed as I am, I must admit to having mastered the dubious art of complaining, always wishing I had more of this, less of that, and generally forgetting that I have precisely what I need. I just have to dig in, make do, and follow the light. And you know what else I think? I think those small pink flowers are the Universe's way of saying "Hey. Get a grip, will ya?"

Just want to say thanks…

The Kid Across the Street

There's this kid across the street. His favorite toy is a scooter, which he can play with for hours on end. And he doesn't just ride the thing — he *works* it, racing with phantom playmates, throwing in motorcycle sound effects, carrying on whole conversations about who won and who lost, and giggling loudly at his own imaginings. Makes me laugh, too.

I remember doing that, only I didn't have a scooter. I had a whole class full of make-believe students that I, their teacher, would lead out to recess — a plastic whistle hanging around my neck, my Mom's old high heels on my feet, and two pairs of my Dad's socks stuffed strategically into my blouse for authenticity. They'd play while I wandered around the front yard, blowing that whistle and calling out gentle admonitions to kids as real to me as the names I given them. Then the bell (a bell only I could hear) would ring, and in we'd march, single file — back to the schoolroom in my mind.

I bet we've all had "a kid across the street." I also bet everyone has been one!

It's one of life's little wonders…

Happy Hanukkah

Ever since I was a little girl, my life has been blessed with an abundance of Jewish friends — and not surprisingly, this time of year always found us exchanging not only gifts and greetings but insights into our different religious beliefs and traditions.

I learned about the Maccabees and the miracle of the Hanukkah oil. I sampled tasty knishes, cheese latkes, and hearty beef brisket. I played games with a little top called a *dreidel*. And I listened to beautiful Hanukkah songs and prayers in Hebrew, which I may not have understood with my head but certainly felt with my heart.

They, in turn, came over to see our Christmas tree and eat as many Santa cookies and candy canes as my mother would allow, while I regaled them with who was who in my manger scene — right down to the donkey. Once, I even taught my friend Sara *Jesus Loves Me This I Know*, which she promptly went home and sang to her grandpa "Zayde," who was both Orthodox and incredibly devout. I'm told he paled slightly — but the smile never left his face.

Maybe all the sharing we did is why it is my hope that when we die, we find ourselves in a long hallway filled with doors for every faith — all leading to the same room where we can finally be together, at last. Until then, Happy Hanukkah to my Jewish friends.

Khanukkah Same'akh…

It's a Dog's Life

And for anyone who doesn't understand what that means, allow me to explain.

Our dogs sleep in our bed, have their own door leading to their own fenced-in yard, and nosh on homemade apple wedges wrapped in chicken, all safely dehydrated and certified healthy by Mom. They spend hours on the back of the family-room couch, watching life go by through double floor-to-ceiling windows — the canine equivalent of a big-screen TV. They hit the dog park every noon with whichever of us is free to accompany them. And the rest of the day is pretty much naps, belly scratches, and more naps. Are they spoiled? Yes. Are we idiots? No. Take bedtime.

Every night, our two goofballs hide underneath the bed (otherwise known as *The Club House*) and wait for us to line up their cookies right at the edge of the bed skirt. We then watch as that skirt flutters slightly while one treat after another disappears. Never do we see a nose, much less a mouth! Honestly, it looks for all the world like that dust ruffle is eating them — which is *our* bedtime treat! And what a treat it is!

Bottom line? Our two pups may be leading *A Dog's Life,* but so are we. And you know something else?

It's saved us a fortune in anti-depressants….

Enjoy Your Trip?

That's one of my husband's favorite expressions — and not because we travel but because his wife is a klutz.

Last night, with guests watching, I caught my toe on a table, tipping over a full glass of wine onto my shoes, whose slippery soles then sent me sliding across the floor. The day before, I somehow managed to step on my own flip flop, nearly launching myself head first into the ground. And there was that time I jumped up to answer the phone after I'd been sitting on my foot.

Having fallen asleep, it rolled under like a numb blob. I might even have though that stupid appendage entirely boneless, had it not been for the distinct sound of breadsticks snapping. Well, thrown off balance, I crashed into the heavy, cast-iron, looks-just-like-real-fire electric stove, on which sat the big screen TV, taking both over with me.

Later, I shared the story with my husband. "Wow. Must hurt." he said, staring at my purple foot. "Yeah. It's busted." Then I watched, thoroughly amused, as he waited for what he hoped might be the appropriate amount of time before daring to ask the really important question, which was "Does the TV still work?" I'm pleased to report it took almost 20 seconds.

But then he's had practice…

In Sympathy and Hope

I had a funny story ready to go for this week's column — my last before Christmas. But given the tragedy in Newtown, what I wrote couldn't seem less important. What matters now are the truly innocent lives stolen by a mind so horribly twisted that it became evil in its capacity for cruelty.

I don't know how those left behind will find their way through such profound grief toward anything resembling *normal*. But they will. Just as the sun always rises no matter how dark the night, so time will heal even the most shattered spirit, especially when accompanied by the love and prayers of an entire world.

What I hope is that faith in the steadfast presence of a benevolent Divinity is not lost in the anger and anguish of this unspeakable horror. Just as we cannot see the wind — only proof of its existence in the movement of leaves and grass and otherwise still waters, neither can we see Him — only evidence that He is forever with us in the miracle of life itself.

And while many wonder where God was last Friday, my heart tells me that he was right there at the Sandy Hook Elementary School, gently gathering souls into His loving arms for the journey homeward — and quietly weeping…

What Goes Up Must Come Down

It sounded like a good idea. We'd take the dogs for a nice long walk somewhere new. Somewhere none of us had ever been. Somewhere with fresh views and different scents. Somewhere invigorating…stimulating. And somewhere flat. So off we went to explore a park that sits atop a nearby mountain — *mountain* being a relative term.

Well, it turns out that the park didn't actually sit atop that mountain. Fact is, the entrance was barely half way up, so after an hour of climbing (*climbing* being another relative term), we asked several people on their way down just how far it was to the top where the trail doubled back — and when they all said "a ways" (which was *much* too relative a term), we gave up.

We blamed it on the dogs, of course. But as we loaded our weary selves into the car, I said, "I think we might be getting old" — to which my husband, obviously not grasping the rhetorical nature of that comment, responded, "*Getting*? HA!" Hey. All I can say is thank heavens "old" is such a relative term.

It is, isn't it…

The Blessing of Spaghetti

I have reached a new low. I am sick of my own cooking. It's not surprising really. After all, I've been cooking for myself since I moved into my first little apartment when I was a senior in college. My specialty then was chicken. It was also all I knew how to cook.

Well, since then, my repertoire has grown enormously, and if I put my mind to it, I could probably go nearly two months without repeating a dinner. But that still means that almost every meal I've ever made I've made hundreds of times — and frankly, I'm sick of them all. *Especially* chicken. Chicken in all the many variations I have come up with. Chicken as cooked à la Martha Stewart, Fannie Farmer, a lifetime of Good Housekeeping magazine recipes, and tips from friends and relatives who are far better cooks than I.

But there is one blessing at this sad juncture in my life. Spaghetti. Plain old spaghetti. I never tire of spaghetti — and neither does my husband, so when late afternoon arrives and I just don't have it in me to be clever, I know that all I have to say is "So…what do you want me to make for dinner? Spaghetti or reservations?" and his answer will always be "Spaghetti!"

Talk about using your noodle…

Sleeping with a Skunk

Yet another confession: I sleep with a skunk. His name is *Mr. Skunky*, and he's my little dog Emily's very best friend — well, next to Jacob, her brother, who is as mystified by her fawning over Mr. Skunky as I am by people who follow the Kardashians.

Mr. Skunky is kind of a seedy looking fella, having been dragged around the house for a long time now — not to mention dropped in water bowls, licked to death, and lost among the dust bunnies under couches from time to time. But every night, just after we get into bed, down goes Emily into the family room to get Mr. Skunky. Then up she comes with that poor old boy in her mouth, after which she drops him in my lap to make my magic.

You see, Mr. Skunky has two squeakers which she has never figured out how to squeak, so when I lift him gently and start squeaking both squeakers at once, her eyes light up, her tail starts wagging, and she tilts her head in awe, much as I do when I watch a concert pianist's fingers glide over the keyboard or see a ballerina rise "en pointe," almost weightless. Then she goes to sleep quite happy, Mr. Skunky by her side — the two of them by mine.

It's not much of a gift, I admit. But the silly wonder I create from this tiny, ragged little toy is pure joy for both of us — indeed, for all of us in that crowded bed.

And joy is always good…

Smooth Talkers

Having spent most of my career working for advertising agencies, I've certainly written my share of ads for *new and improved* products — always assured by the creative director who was assured by the account rep who was assured by the client that there *was*, indeed, something *new and improved* about them. Maybe that's why the cosmetics industry is getting on my nerves.

I watch TV ads for moisturizers featuring a 22-year-old model staring in the mirror at herself, aglow at how incredible she looks after beginning her new beauty regimen with that particular moisturizer, when the fact is that she couldn't find a wrinkle on her face with an electron microscope.

Likewise, I see print ads for moisturizers making that same promise — only to notice that in the before picture, replete with crow's feet and laugh lines, the model is grinning like a fool, while in the after picture, her smile is gone — and with it the crow's feet and laugh lines. My take? Why bother with pricey face creams when being grumpy is so effective!

So here's my message for the cosmetics industry: We older gals may be wrinkly, but we're not stupid. Show us the courtesy of a little honesty, please. And while you're at it, hurry up and invent something that actually works.

We're also not getting any younger…

The Children Between the Headlines

Not long ago, a beautiful little girl I know died quietly at home in her childhood bedroom, waiting until everyone was busy elsewhere to close her eyes to this world and open them to the next. Some would say she died peacefully. And it's true that there were no bullets or sirens or headlines involved. But her struggle with cancer was long and painful, demanding of her and those who loved her extraordinary courage and grace.

You see, the truth is, children die every day. They die from car accidents and falls and neglect and abuse. They die from drugs and suicide. And they die from diseases we can't yet cure. But except for their names and photos on the obituary page of their local papers, such children are rarely news. Just kids who died.

Except there is no such thing as *just kids who died*. All children are headlines to someone. So while we cannot protect children from everything, we can certainly do better, seizing the opportunities before us to advocate, donate, and volunteer on their behalf. And not just when a headline prompts — and sometimes even shames us — into doing so, but every single day, because each of us is capable of preventing one accident or fall, stopping one incident of neglect or abuse, saving one kid from taking drugs or his own life, or playing at least a tiny part in achieving one breakthrough on one disease.

In loving memory of both the children in the headlines and those in between, we must...

Technologeez!

Last week, my computer — just six weeks past its warrantee — died. With a tiny little whir and very gentle click, it went silent and very dark. Forever and ever. Amen.

Now, I'm not complaining, having recently vowed to curtail that habit. But I would like to share (sharing being different than complaining) that first I had to replace the computer itself, which was, as I believe I noted, just six weeks over warrantee (ka-ching), after which I had to upgrade my software so everything is compatible (ka-ching), and then I had to pay someone with the brains to have majored in computer technology to crack into that lifeless six-weeks-out-of-warrantee laptop (ka-ching), retrieve whatever could be retrieved (ka-ching), and do it quickly (ka-ching, ka-ching, ka-ching). And I had no choice.

As a writer, losing my computer is like Picasso losing his brush. OK, maybe that comparison is a little too grand, so let's just go with a housepainter losing his roller. But it does make every ka-ching an irritating necessity — especially six weeks past the warrantee. (Yes, six. Did I mention that?) Not that I'm complaining.

I'm just sharing…

Fried Green Tomato

That's right, tomato. As in one.

The saga, such as it is, began back in May, when a generous friend, who is also an outstanding gardener, gave me a tomato plant, the care and tending of which I took very seriously. Indeed, I went out, bought a nice big pot, planted my crop, and — watering can at the ready — awaited my August harvest. Then we decided to have the house power washed.

Now, you would have thought it might have occurred to me that there'd be something besides water dispatching all that mold and algae on our house as swiftly and completely as it did. But no. I thought the *power* did the work — until two days later when most of the plants in my front garden and window boxes began a slow, agonizing shrivel. And when I checked my tomato plant, it was totally withered, too — except for one tiny green tomato, only slightly singed, clinging to one bedraggled shoot.

Well, I picked that poor little orphan — my one fried green tomato — and in an act of contrition for having been too stupid to protect it, I placed it on a plate, where it sits even now, staring at me with contempt. Of course, I could be imagining the staring part. I mean, a vegetable can't really stare, now can it? But I sure don't plan to eat it.

It's been through enough already…

Weighty Thoughts

Years ago, when I first became a step-Mom, my new daughter — just ten years my junior — decided to go on a diet. Well, she measured and planned, counting calories and grams of this and that, and generally consigning over her whole day to the preparation and consumption of three less-than-appetizing meals, and I remember thinking how the degree to which she needed to focus on food was self-defeating. I mean, how can you possibly hope to lose weight when your solution requires obsessing over food?

Well, I thought about that the other night as I watched political pundits, Washington insiders, Washington outsiders, Hollywood's elite, and folks on the street — right, left, center, and off-center — all duking it out over the issue of bigotry in America, and I remember thinking how the degree to which we focus on differences is self-defeating. I mean, how can we possibly hope to reduce prejudice when our solution requires obsessing over distinctions.

I could be wrong. I often am. But I do know this: My step-daughter looks great, now that she's stopped counting calories.

Maybe we could all learn something from that…

Aha!

I believe I have just solved one of life's tiny mysteries. It seems the difference between low-cost store-brand foods and the pricier name-brand labels isn't the quality of the food. It's quality of the packaging.

The other night, that store-brand box of fries that said *press to open* wouldn't open no matter how much I pressed. And last night, the handy dandy tab on the top of the store-brand soup — you know, the one you're supposed to simply lift and pull— broke right off, which wouldn't have been a big deal except that even with a shiny new can opener, I couldn't get in. I might as well have been trying to rip it apart with toe-nail clippers. (Ew. I just grossed myself out.)

And don't count on resealing anything, either. Once you've ripped store-brand packaging six ways from Sunday, that little zip-lock thingy now lying on the floor isn't going to do you much good. Just keep reminding yourself how much you saved and grab some scotch tape or a good old twist tie from the junk drawer.

They'll be right next to the scissors you used to open that bag with the convenient tear-open top…

The Switch

I've always thought that fall is a season quite aptly named. After all, the leaves fall…the temperature falls…and, for a while anyway, my spirits do, too. But I seem to have this internal switch, maybe even primeval — and once it gets thrown by that first truly crisp morning, fall becomes as welcome as any other change of season

Last week, that switch was thrown by a breeze that was not only cool but dry, and within seconds, I found myself thinking about planting a few bright yellow mums and baking the apple pie for which I have become known — a high-calorie artery clogger that turns fruit into actual candy. I even began imagining packing away the well-worn collection of t-shirts that had served as my uniform since the last time there was a cool, dry breeze!

I was premature, of course. The breeze didn't last. Indeed, the humidity returned in spades. But with the switch successfully thrown, I am now ready to welcome fall whenever it truly arrives. Just not winter.

Not yet…

Weeds and Wildflowers

As a lifelong contrarian, I guess it figures that I love weeds! But really — the flowering kinds are simply beautiful, like the Oxeye Daisies that grow in large stands every June and the pink and white Dame's Rocket that blossoms at nearly the same time. I even love Queen Anne's Lace, despite the fact that it *does* make me sneeze! And there's another reason I love weeds.

When found in the actual woods, and not along the roadside where they might belong to someone, they are free for the picking! Indeed, I gather them all summer, right along with wildflowers, enjoying them every bit as much as the cutting flowers I grow in my back garden — maybe even more, they being heaven sent. And the smallest are my favorites.

I keep a bouquet of miniatures in a tiny white vase beside my kitchen sink. Have for years. And it's not just the flowers themselves that I love. It's the memory of the walk on which they were picked.

Makes me smile…

Seeing is Relieving

I swear, you can find anything on the Internet. For example, the other day, I read that the easiest way to keep ice cream from dripping out the bottom of a cone is to tuck a small marshmallow in before scooping on the fudge ripple. And shortly after that, I learned that if you have some leftover wine at the end of a special evening, you can freeze it in ice cube trays for use in soups and sauces at another time — a very helpful tip for anyone who actually *has* leftover wine now and then. I do not.

Then yesterday, a favorite cousin sent us a cool *YouTube* video demonstrating how to test batteries without a battery tester. Seems you just hold one a couple of inches above a tabletop or counter — flat end down — then drop it. If it wobbles and falls over, it's shot. But if it lands with a thud and remains upright, it's a keeper. How easy is that — and how great! I mean, we have totally dead, almost dead, half dead, useable in a pinch, nearly good, and good batteries everywhere!

Just imagine the square footage I'll be able to free up when I find out which is which…

The Nightly Ews

I am not quick to fall asleep. While my husband loses consciousness when he smells percale sheets, I can lie awake for hours — hence my attachment to the remote and late-night TV.

On a good night, I can watch four sitcoms at the same time, clicking around strategically enough to follow what's happening without actually getting invested. But recently, I watched a couple of low-budget, bad-script, fake-blood, horror flicks — one featuring giant crocodiles and the other a particularly ridiculous-looking snow monster. Why?

Well, to tell you the truth, trying to turn them off was like trying to pass a car crash without staring. I simply couldn't. But I also discovered that I could doze off for five…sometimes ten minutes and it really didn't matter, making them, well…an insomniac's dream! (Hey! Sleep is sleep!)

Am I concerned about watching such drivel? Not even a little. At that time of night, TV is pretty much all drivel. Am I excited about tuning in to this weekend's *Sharknado* (please don't ask) marathon? I'd say no — not even remotely.

But you know, I sure could use the rest…

Infinity and Plastic Wrap

Nearly eight years ago, my sister-in-law gave me a really big box of plastic wrap — you know, the kind you buy at a really big-box store, where things only come in two sizes: huge and gargantuan. Well, it's too weird. I've used that plastic wrap steadily during each of those eight years, and it's still not gone. Not even close.

No one believes me, but it's true. I've wrapped and wrapped and wrapped my way through countless holidays, birthday dinners, and barbeques — not to mention a significant portion of two American presidencies, and that roll just won't quit. Sometimes, it actually gives me the creeps. I mean, maybe there's a time warp in that cabinet — or a strange molecular phenomenon of some kind.

Truth is, if I could pick what I want to self-perpetuate or regenerate or whatever is going on in that kitchen cabinet, it would be cookies. We're always running out of cookies. Or Chardonnay — which disappears pretty quickly around here. Or cash! Now that would be great. You pay a bill, and poof — the money's back!

Well, I could go on forever — not unlike that roll. But alas, the only thing I can't seem to run out of around here is that plastic wrap.

Foiled again…

...And Yet, We Still Live in New England

Yes. That was the subject line of the email that I sent out last Saturday with some post-storm photographs of just what a 36-inch snowfall actually looks like. Most commiserated. A few laughed. And one cousin in Florida responded by noting that she and the family were heading out for a day on their boat. (Thanks.) But really. It does beg the question, "Why do I live in a place where a big chunk of the year is gray, cold, gray, slushy, gray, snowy, gray, windy, and gray." The answer? I live here because my family does — so go ask them.

OK, seriously. New England is, by and large, one of the safer places to live weather-wise, and we all know it. I mean, we can pretty much count on having only hurricanes and snowstorms — both of which come with all kinds of advance warning involving all sorts of high drama that begins the second a blip on the radar appears in Siberia. So here we all stay, fairly certain that if all hell is about to break loose, an extra loaf of bread will save the day.

Oh, and there's one more plus. Having survived shoveling 36 inches of snow, the effective equivalent of a stress test, I have earned the right to get myself a box of really greasy doughnuts and some cheese twists — fried, not baked. And I will.

As soon as I'm able to move…

Why Is It?

Why is it that whenever I find myself stuck in a line of traffic moving at the speed of a garden slug on a one-lane road in the middle of nowhere, the pace car always seems to make it through the one stoplight within fifty miles, leaving the rest of us to wait? And why is it that stoplights in the middle of nowhere seem to last so long?

Why is it that attempting to match colors from memory is guaranteed to fail, yet I continue to do it? And why is it that when something I've insisted on color matching from memory doesn't match, I'm still surprised?

Why is it that I can calculate the per-unit price of any item in the grocery store in my head while singing along to seventies hits on the PA system, yet I cannot balance my checkbook without a calculator, wine, Kleenex, and my husband? And why is it that I even bother when my bank has far more technology and an auditor?

And lastly (for now), why is it I'm careful to buy four totally separate bananas a week in various stages of ripening, then find myself forced to eat them all at once because somehow they catch up with each other, making their final turn into mush on the exact same day?

Mysteries like these keep me sharp. Or just confused.

I don't know which…

The Late Judith Henderson

The other day I watched as a perfectly splendid formation of geese flew overhead, obviously headed south — but all I could think was, "It's February! Aren't they a little behind schedule?" And that's when it occurred to me that those geese and I have a lot in common.

I am always a little behind schedule, developing a taste for new fashion trends at just about the time they go out of style, getting hooked on new TV shows the day before the cast — anxious to take on other creative projects after such a long, long run — agree to call it quits, and discovering that the "guess whats" I add to any given conversation aren't news to anyone else. And that's not the worst.

The worst is that not only do I have no sense of timing but no sense of time. My "be there in a minute" should really be more like "be there in 15 minutes," thanks to a flawed inner clock that seems to register the passing of time in quarter-hour increments. As a result, I am rarely *where* I should be *when* I should be, thus usually on the fly just like those geese — with one important difference.

They can only be late twice a year…

Heart Lines

Not to be morose, but the truth is that when your parents have gone on, as all parents do sooner or later, it feels a lot like being a kid lost at the circus. Sure, you're surrounded by people, but not the familiar faces with whom you arrived — the faces you trust to watch over you, to make everything right, and to love you no matter what.

I've been thinking about that lately — probably because my Dad died 24 years ago this week, and Mom nine years ago next month. But I've also been thinking about what I've learned since their going, which is this: While bloodlines may define one's original family, it is heart lines that unite us with the in-laws, cousins, steps, friends, neighbors, and even longtime colleagues who become our extended family as we grow older, because family, no matter how it occurs, is everything. Truth is, that's all I could think about last Sunday, as mine gathered for dinner.

My niece brought her terrific "young man" for his second official holiday, giving us all kinds of new things to talk and smile about. My step-daughter has a new beau of her own, who wasn't there but will likely turn up soon. And our family recently welcomed a little baby girl, who — being both beautiful and spirited — is destined to break hearts and probably a few rules! We may not be related by blood, but we will be by love. Indeed, chairs long empty are filling up again, and what a welcome thing that is!

There's nothing like the joyful noise and commotion of a packed house to quiet the heart...

Well, This Could Spell Trouble

Recently — indeed, not long after getting my new computer, I was typing a simple email only to notice that words were lighting up, then changing. For example, I had written "How awesome!" yet what was on the screen had morphed into "How awful!" Likewise, I had written, "Please email me if you have any questions" only to read "Please empale me if you have any questions" — *empale* being a seldom-used version of the word *impale*, which means to pierce through with a sharp object! What?!?!?!?!?

Turns out, I have some new software that not only checks spelling automatically but *corrects* spelling automatically — which would be awesome (not awful) if that software had clue one as to what I intended to say. But it doesn't. It simply finds a misspelled word, then grabs another with a similar spelling and pops it in — which is awful (not awesome).

Suffice it to say, I will not be typing "lots of luck" any time soon, lest one or two of those letters get mixed up and that crazy spellcheck kicks in.

Holy shot…

I'll Be Back

And not just because I believe in reincarnation but because I have always, always wanted to be a back-up singer in a rock and roll band, and that just wasn't possible this time around.

Mostly it had to do with the lack of a good singing voice. But there's also the small matter of my wrinkled knees, which has made wearing the kind of little black dress I'd want to wear ill-advised, despite the fact that I'd probably be belting out my harmonies pretty much in the dark at a mike a little to the right of the drummer — and way behind several guitarists, someone on keyboards, and amps stacked so high I could only be seen from the second balcony anyway.

So, look for me. Not soon, but eventually. I'll be the back-up singer in the little black dress with the great knees a little to the right of the drummer — and, well…you know the rest. At least, I hope I will.

If there's a mix-up, I could end up being the balding roadie with the snake tattoos…

Canine Sleep Deprivation

It's not what you think. My dogs sleep well — and often, which probably accounts for a certain middle-of-the-night restlessness on their part that's wrecking havoc with *my* sleep. Take last night.

I turned off the light at 10, mindful of an early morning appointment — but half an hour later, Emily decides to take the shortcut across my chest on her way to the floor to get a drink of water, waking her brother Jacob, who gets his own drink of water and then starts licking his paw, which he's not supposed to do, thus necessitating a brief chat between him and me. I am now wide awake.

At 11:30, apparently concerned that Mr. Skunky — the favorite toy with which she sleeps— might be lonely, Emily walks over me again on her way off the bed and downstairs to root around in the toy basket for her squeaky bone, which she not only brings back up and onto the bed but digs a hole for in the sheets before getting back down for another few sips of water, thus arousing Jacob, who gets his own drink and returns to licking his paw. I am now wide awake. Again.

Around 1 a.m., all the water Emily has consumed calls for a quick visit to the doggy yard, which my husband graciously oversees. But when she returns, she gets into Jacob's bed, to which he takes exception. Now everyone is wide awake — which is probably just as well, since it's Jake's turn to go out and my turn to assist.

I know. It's our own fault. We need to be tougher. But it's hard, because they are so sweet — especially when they are sleeping, which is, of course, what they do all day.

After all, they're up all night…

So I Said to My Husband...

"...what should we do for our anniversary this year?" and he replied, "When is it?" Yup. He really did. And as we all know, that is *not* a good answer to that question. But the truth is, I thought his response was pretty amusing. Brave, yes — but also amusing, and I thought it was amusing because odd things amuse me.

The other day, I was stopped at a light when a big white truck drove by. It had a huge fish painted on the side, and underneath it said, MEAT WITHOUT FEET. Well, I thought about that, and it got me laughing. In fact, I got this mental image of some guy wracking his brain for a company name, only to come up with "Fred's Filets" or "From Sea to Shining Seafoods." But not these folks! No siree! They are MEAT WITHOUT FEET, and for all that might be plain and simple about that name, it's not only perfect, but perfectly hilarious.

Another example is a bumper sticker that I actually ordered online because I found it so funny. It says, "Horn broken. Watch for finger." Still makes me laugh. Of course, I didn't put it on the car. As my husband is quick to point out, I have my standards. They may be low — but I have them.

What a guy...

Forget the NSA

I'm worried about the lady who lives in the self-check-out scanner at my grocery store. You know, the one who's always telling everyone that "the bagging area is full…" or to "please move your red seedless grapes to the belt." I'm telling you, that woman knows more about me than the NSA on a good day.

I mean, I barely arrive and I hear, "Welcome!" followed by reminders to swipe my store card and exercise regularly. (OK, I made up the thing about exercising — but still.) And yesterday, she kept instructing me to "remove all items from the scanner scale." Well, "Ha!" I thought to myself. "I don't have any items on your stupid scanner scale…" only to discover that the tie string at the bottom of my sweatshirt was indeed brushing her precious scale! And if you think that's bad, consider this.

The coupons she pumps out reveal just how much information she's gathered on my buying habits. I mean, she not only knows that I color my hair but which kind of hair color I use. And recently, she kicked out a coupon for an entirely different brand — one that I've never tried, as if to say, "Checked a mirror lately?" I tell you, it's freaky.

So as far as I'm concerned, the NSA can dig up whatever they want on me. They still won't know the half of it until they talk to her. But if they do, they'd better not try using an expired coupon.

That woman knows everything…

My New Years Resolutions

I don't have any. Not a one. And that's because I've learned. The second I decide I *shouldn't* do something anymore, I want to do it more than anything else in the world — and as much as possible. Likewise, the minute I decide I *should* do more of something, I have no desire to — no matter what it is.

Of course, that's not to say that I don't try to be the best person I can be every single day, because I do. I arise every morning and — like the bumper sticker — say "Lord, keep your arm around my shoulder and your hand over my mouth," my mouth being what tends to get me into the most trouble. But if I get too specific, things go awry.

Decades ago, when I was a smoker, I decided I should quit through hypnosis. Well, no sooner had I heard the words "You will not smoke" than I thought to myself "Wanna bet?" And needless to say, I continued to light up, stopping only when my husband introduced me to his brand new cardiologist — in the ER.

And so, as we round the bend into 2013, I have no New Years resolutions to report. The best I can do is renew my commitment to making the most of what I consider to be an incredibly blessed life.

That alone should keep me very busy…

Cents and Sensibility

I used to love grocery coupons. I'd clip a few 99-centers, then combine them with double or triple store coupons, saving $1.98 — and sometimes a whopping $2.97 — on a single item! Always made me feel like I'd outsmarted someone somewhere!

Then it all seemed to end, with the 99-cent coupons becoming dollar coupons, which cannot be doubled or tripled…the double and triple coupons disappearing… and the dollar coupons becoming buy-two-get-a-buck-off coupons — then buy-three-get-a-buck-off coupons, turning a simple purchase into a freakin' investment with a paltry per-unit discount of just 33¢!

Well, maybe the manufacturers don't get it, but the grocery stores sure do, because about the time I'd given up on saving anything anywhere anymore, my local market started holding buy-one-get-two-free sales — which is like a 99-cent-off-plus-triple-coupon deal on steroids. Of course, I did need to buy some new shelves and a freezer to hold all the get-two-free extras. But who cares. Those sales have me back to feeling like I'm outsmarting someone somewhere.

That's a real saving grace in this otherwise bleak economy…

The First Day of Spring

The 2013 calendar says that the first day of spring was March 20th, but for me, it was last Thursday, when the dogs and I took our daily walk in the woods only to find that finally — finally! — our little forest was awakening with life.

The trees and underbrush wore a misting of pale green so diffuse as to be almost not there, while peeking out from beneath dead, decaying leaves were young sprouts of this and that, all huddled together in clusters of chartreuse and lime and jade. It was subtle, but at long last, winter's relentless palette of cold grays and sodden browns was yielding to an increasingly insistent sun, and it all looked and felt so good.

Well, yesterday, we discovered small stands of Yellow Trillium and Purple Deadnettle alongside the trail that had literally popped up overnight — and when we started off on today's woodland wander, we were greeted by a parade of Quaker Ladies, miniscule blue flowers that look as if they were made for tiny elfin creatures to gather in tiny elfin arms to take home to tiny elfin cottages. Then, we saw them!

Laying claim to sunlit patches everywhere were Dandelions by the dozen! And while these fearless denizens of wherever their seeds happen to alight may be the scourge of lawn lovers everywhere, who could possibly fail to welcome a brilliant yellow flower standing proudly, face to the sky, declaring for anyone not yet convinced that spring has begun!

Not me, boy! Not me…

The Bottom-Shelf Rancid-Red Blues

I started drinking a glass of wine every night at 6:00 when I started working from home — that first sip being the line of demarcation between the official work day and all the other work I do after the official work day. And I must say, I have grown to look forward to that glass of wine with what I have often wondered might not be excessive anticipation.

"I'm turning into a wino," I told my husband one night, when I had treated myself to a couple of extra splashes and was feeling a little guilty. "Nah," he said. "You can't become a wino on a budget of $7.99 a week. Besides, you have no tolerance." And it's true. I can't get past that one glass — two if I'm snacking. But I really felt better this week, when I bought a *really* cheap bottle of Merlot.

I found it on the bottom shelf at my liquor store, where all the really crummy stuff gathers dust (literally) and it was so nasty, I couldn't drink it. I mean, I wanted to. It was, after all, 6:00 p.m. But there was simply no way, so I poured the whole bottle into the kitchen sink.

"Couldn't you have made salad dressing with it or something?" asked my husband. "No," I said, "It was too awful." But believe me, I'm not singin' the Bottom-Shelf Rancid-Red Blues. That dreadful wine proved to me that I can't drink simply for sake of drinking.

And you know, I think that drain is running better, too…

Meandering the Mall

I don't know quite what happened. First, we had strip malls, where storefronts all faced a parking lot. Then suddenly everything moved inside into immense, cavernous spaces requiring giant maps, clocks with several time zones, and some serious stamina. Now poof! We're back to strip malls — except now the stores don't face a parking lot but more stores, with a small street running in between. The result? *Mall meandering*, a new phenomenon which involves preoccupied shoppers roaming from one side of the street to the other pretty much anywhere, often without looking, and usually without so much as an "oops-I-didn't-see-you-coming-thanks-for-not-running-me-over" wave or nod.

Yes. I know. My sarcasm is showing. Pedestrians do trump cars. They always have, they always will, and I am keenly aware of that fact, which is why I take those quaint little driving lanes at a crawl — knuckles white…eyes peeled…stomach churning…insurance papers handy. But with official pedestrian crossings provided every 25 yards, is it really necessary for those having the right of way to exercise it every three feet — and without warning?

And until cars are made of nerf, is it really all that smart…

Thy Rod and Thy Staff — and Hal, They Comfort Me

Yup. Those words are part of the 23rd Psalm all right — well, except the part about Hal. But for 38 years, my veterinary hospital has been the answer to many a prayer for me and my critters, so I don't think God will mind a little copyright infringement!

My first visit there was in 1974, when everything was brand new — the waiting room…the reception desk…even a fresh-faced veterinarian named Rod. I was there with Woofer, a sad little stray we found huddled under a mailbox in a thunderstorm. And ever since, Rod and his staff — and a relative newcomer named Hal — have watched over a succession of beloved dogs, one very dear cat, and a couple of foster puppies, one of which was adopted right out of my arms as I walked in the door by Rod's sister!

During those years, I learned a lot. I learned that "providing a sample" doesn't mean delivering the whole enchilada in a coffee can. I learned that male Bichons who have been neutered can still be pretty quick on the draw yet very poor at reholstering — an episode that left the entire place howling and for which I was not charged. And I learned that giving a dog a pill calls for peanut butter, while giving a cat a pill calls for band-aids. Above all, I learned that even when you think all is lost, it's not — and that relationships matter.

Along the way, there have been a lot of laughs, and there have been a few inevitable tears. But mostly, there has been the profound peace of mind that comes with knowing that when I dial that familiar phone number, whoever answers will say Hopmeadow Animal Hospital — not Ramona's Artificial Nail Emporium and Sandwich Shop — and everything will be OK.

And so, I want to say thank you to that wonderful place for many lifetimes of blessings. Thy Rod and thy staff — and yes, Hal — have indeed comforted me.

I am grateful…

Deck the Halls with Boughs of Holly?

Sure. Way back when, maybe. But these days, you need a degree in electrical engineering and a box of wine to get the job done!

Yesterday, I spent hours untangling heaven knows how many linear feet of tiny white lights (don't go there...I absolutely *did* wind them carefully last January), locating the three or four dead bulbs interrupting the flow of juice to the rest, tethering this arguably vast network of strands to the house via an equally vast network of extension cords, then arranging the whole twinkling mess into precise, twelve-inch swags along the entire wraparound porch railing. Next came the window candles with their extension cords, the lighted wreath and miniature trees by the front door with their extension cords, and last, but never least, the Christmas tree itself with — yes! — several more extension cords.

So why do I go through all this when a couple of boughs of holly would do it? Because it looks lovely. And because it reminds me of my childhood home. Besides, with every outlet in my house now officially spoken for, vacuuming is a virtual impossibility until at least January 2nd!

Merry Christmas to me...

Nobody Touches the Krud Kutter

When we moved a couple of years back, things got very weird for a while. I missed my neighbors and my garden. I even missed my mailman. But I also missed my systems. Hey — spontaneous as we like to think we all are, most of us have systems. At least, I do.

For instance, we always threw our dirty clothes into the hamper in the bathroom — until our new bathroom didn't have room for the hamper, at which point you would have thought some great cosmic finger had just poked my little ant hill, the way I ran around trying to figure out what to do with those dirty clothes. And that was nothing compared to the confusion of moving all the pots and pans and dishes into a new kitchen. It was like waking up to find my feet sewn to my nose.

Not surprisingly, new systems have evolved. But I also like to think I've learned how to be more relaxed about things, too. For example, ever since my husband pointed out that if, when pulling the car into the garage, I line up the Krud Kutter on the shelf with my shoulder, I won't keep smashing into the lawn mower, I've been good to go — and really, so much more relaxed. It's amazing.

I just hope we never need to clean our gutters, because nobody, and I mean *nobody*, touches that Krud Kutter…

The Laundry on the Stairs

After folding laundry last night, I took the pile and placed it on the stairs. I always do. So does my husband, and so did our parents and theirs. I wonder how many people do that — you know, leave their folded laundry on the stairs for the next person heading up to carry with them. Got me to thinking about all the silly, lovely little habits we learn from our elders and pass on to our kids.

I have a green thumb like two grandmothers and an aunt. I enjoy classical music and bawdy jokes, just like my Dad. And I sit exactly the way my Mom always sat — shoes off…one leg under for a cushion.

My older brother's handwriting is just like my Dad's, as is the warm smile that spreads slowly across his face like the sun coming out whenever he's amused! But his sharp, dry wit comes straight from our mother, along with his taste for iced tea and crosswords.

And we used to think our younger brother, who looks nothing like us, might have had something to do with the milk man — until we saw a grainy, black and white home movie of my parents when they were very young, and there he was! An exact reprise of our Dad — and not just in looks but in gestures.

It guess it's no big surprise. Between nature and nurture, likeness happens. But what a blessing to have such tiny, precious bits of continuity in our lives.

And how lovely to get such comfort from laundry…

Late Life Lyrics

I love to sing along to the radio, CDs, my iShuffle, whatever. I hear music and I sing. And I've written about this habit before — largely because it doesn't always bring quite as much joy to those within earshot as it does to me. But I mention it again because something magnificent is happening.

You know how there are always these lines in certain songs that you can't quite make out? Well, with my new ear buds, I am now deciphering lyrics I'd never really understood before — lyrics I routinely mumbled during my sing-alongs, as well as lyrics I had always mistaken for something entirely different.

I mean, finally, I have a clue as to what's going on in *Jumpin' Jack Flash.* I can now make it through the Hollies' *Long Cool Woman In a Black Dress* without sounding like a complete dolt. And I always thought Bobby Vinton was singing "roses are red my love, my lips are blue" — which sort of makes sense, his lips missing her as much as he might be. But it's not "my lips are blue." It's "violets are blue," just like it has *always* been "violets are blue." Yeesh.

Anyway, every day now, I discover some new and wonderful lyric I've been stumbling over for years, making my performances much more authentic, if nothing else. Well, for the most part.

I will never unravel *Louie Louie*...

Thesaurus Anyone?

I watch a lot of news — and I mean a lot, mostly because like to stay informed. But it's getting more and more irritating every day. And not just the news itself but the complete lack of originality shown by elected officials and the media when communicating with the rest of us.

This growing deficiency was most recently evidenced by the incessant use of the cliché "kicking the can down the road" in lieu of equally appropriate — indeed *more* appropriate — words like *postpone*, *delay*, *avoid*, *defer*, *put off*, *dodge*, *sidestep*, *duck*, or *evade* during the most recent budget debates. I'm not sure why it became the *de facto* metaphor for the act of failing to act, but here's my fear.

Pretty soon, kids everywhere will be accusing parents who dare to utter those hated words "we'll see" of "kicking the can down the road" — and when they do, I guarantee some cans *will* be kicked. Metaphorically, of course.

No butts about it…

In the Black

When I got up Easter morning and went to the closet to choose something springy and colorful to wear, I was genuinely startled to realize that I own no less than four pairs of black dress pants. I mean, I knew I did — at least in that vague way most of us know what's sitting in our closet. But it made me wonder. Why *do* I own four pairs of black dress pants?

Well, I think I own four pairs of black dress pants because they are all very different. No, really. They are! Well, maybe not *very* different, but different to the extent that they *can* be. However, I *know* that I own four pairs of black dress pants because everything that matches one pair of black dress pants is likely to match them all, and I am nothing if not frugal. (OK, cheap.)

Still, Easter morning and four pairs of black pants? So I've made a decision. I'm heading out this week to buy a pair of not-black dress pants. Maybe something in khaki or beige or a nice off-white so that everything I already own that matches my black dress pants will also match my not-black dress pants.

Hey. I'm willing to invest in some new clothes, but not if it puts me in the red…

She of the Stupid Hat

As many of you already know, I am not a hat person. I don't wear them in the winter, no matter how cold it is, and I don't wear them in the rain, not matter how wet it is. Why? Hat hair — plain and simple. There isn't a hat in the world that I can wear for ten minutes without looking like someone découpaged my head. Then along came this unbearably hot summer, and I had to give in.

Working outside in the heat made even me, the hat-hater of all time, don a big old straw number with a huge floppy brim. My neighbor, who is very kind, said it looked cute — but it didn't. And as I'd get hotter and the headband would get soggier, it would descend down my forehead and over my ears, making me look like the green-thumb equivalent of Elmer Fudd.

Then one day I was weeding, singing along to my music, and yeah…maybe bouncing my head a little in time to the beat — that stupid hat nearly down to my nose — when I noticed a truck full of guys on their lunch break watching me. I thought they might think I looked kind of funny, but the truth is they weren't laughing. Just staring, which is never good.

Dear god, I hope next summer is cooler…

I'm Thankful for What I *Don't* Have

Sadly, many of us have had a tough year. But with Thanksgiving just days away, we all might do well to remember that sometimes — indeed, often — it's what we *don't* have that should make us truly thankful.

For instance, I don't have a big fancy house or a big fancy car, but that just means that I don't have big fancy property taxes. I don't have credit cards, so I don't have the debt that goes with them. And I don't have enough money to take vacations, which leaves me plenty of time to savor my own little world.

I don't have big dreams — just little ones that come true every day. I don't have a favorite song — just thousands I get to hear all the time. And I don't have tons of friends — just a handful or two of really, really good ones I can always count on.

Above all, I don't have an illness or disability capable of stealing away life's everyday joys — and if those were the only two things I did not have, I would be lucky enough.

So yes, there are lots of things I don't have — and for that I am truly grateful…

Please join me every week at
http://www.westhartfordnews.com/opinion/
for more *Thinking Aloud*.

Made in the USA
Middletown, DE
01 December 2023

43207685R00091